"There are . . . moments of out-and-out hilarity in *Thanks for the Memories* . . . but the out-and-out quickest quipster in this volume is the redoubtable Thomas herself. . . . She has a razor tongue and a rapier wit and an equal-opportunity approach to deploying them."
—*The Washington Post*

"Ms. Thomas focuses on an important aspect of the presidency that has not received sufficient attention from scholars: the role that humor, particularly self-deprecating humor, can play in building public support and public sympathy for a president."
—*Richmond Times-Dispatch*

"Thomas lets us pull up a chair by her ringside seat to history for a glimpse of some of the poignant, funny, and memorable moments she's witnessed in a long career of writing."
—*San Antonio Express-News*

"Funny stuff. But the essence of this book is really Thomas's long and illustrious career as a White House reporter. . . . The book is a sometimes amusing, sometimes insightful postscript to Thomas's . . . 1999 book, *Front Row at the White House.*"
—*The Buffalo News*

"The First Lady of the White House press corps follows up her engaging memoir, *Front Row at the White House,* with a collection of humorous and sometimes touching stories. . . . Thomas here provides some good laughs for these serious times."
—*Library Journal*

"Thomas's memories . . . of these men are indeed telling. . . . Thomas's 'all in good fun' attitude and breadth of experience make this a light but entertaining follow-up to her recent memoir, *Front Row at the White House.*"
—*Publishers Weekly*

ALSO BY HELEN THOMAS

DATELINE: WHITE HOUSE

FRONT ROW AT THE WHITE HOUSE

THANKS FOR THE MEMORIES, MR. PRESIDENT

*Wit and Wisdom from the Front Row
at the White House*

HELEN THOMAS

A LISA DREW BOOK

SCRIBNER

NEW YORK   LONDON   TORONTO   SYDNEY

A LISA DREW BOOK/SCRIBNER
1230 Avenue of the Americas
New York, NY 10020

First Lisa Drew/Scribner trade paperback edition 2003
SCRIBNER and design are trademarks of Macmillan Library Reference USA, Inc.,
used under license by Simon & Schuster, the publisher of this work.

A LISA DREW BOOK is a trademark of Simon & Schuster, Inc.

For information about special discounts for bulk purchases,
please contact Simon & Schuster Special Sales:
1-800-456-6798 or business@simonandschuster.com

Designed by Colin Joh
Text set in Schneidler

Manufactured in the United States of America

3 5 7 9 10 8 6 4

The Library of Congress has cataloged the Scribner edition as follows:
Thomas, Helen, 1920–
Thanks for the memories, Mr. President : wit and wisdom from the
front row at the White House / Helen Thomas.
p. cm.
"A Lisa Drew book."
Includes index.
1. Thomas, Helen, 1920– —Anecdotes. 2. Presidents—United States—Biography—Anecdotes.
3. Presidents—United States—History—20th century—Anecdotes. 4. Presidents—United States—
Quotations. 5. Women journalists—United States—Biography—Anecdotes. 6. United States—
Politics and government—1945–1989—Anecdotes. 7. United States—Politics and
government—1989—Anecdotes.
E176.1.T44 2002
973'.920922—dc21
ISBN 0-7432-0225-2
0-7432-0226-0 (Pbk)

This book is dedicated to all the presidents I've covered, who maintained their sense of humor in the best of times and the worst of times.

And, always, my beloved family.

CONTENTS

Thanks for the Memories, Mr. President

INTRODUCTION

The scene: the White House Correspondents Association annual dinner, April 2000.

Cuing up is the now famous "The Final Days" video detailing how President Clinton is spending his time in the waning days of office.

Cut to press secretary Joe Lockhart, who says, "With the vice president and the first lady out on the campaign trail, things aren't as exciting as they used to be around here. In fact, it's really starting to wind down."

Cut to Clinton standing at the podium in the White House pressroom:

"There's bipartisan support for it in Congress . . . and at least the principles I set out in my State of the Union. If they send me the bill in its present form, I will sign it. Okay, any questions? Helen? [Then a little desperately] *Helen?*"

Camera pans over to me sitting in my chair, my head back. I wake up, lift my head, and see the president standing there: "Are you *still here?*"

A dejected Clinton leaves the podium and the camera follows him out—and in the background you hear Frank Sinatra crooning "One More for the Road."

Well, I'm still here. And, in a manner of speaking, so is Bill Clinton. But only one of us is still working at the White House.

And here it is 2001: I've covered eight chief executives so far, and now I'm breaking in a new one. For a while, Clinton was going to be the last, when I decided to hang up my daily news spurs with UPI in May 2000. But hey, someone has to show these people the ropes, and when Charles J. Lewis, Washington bureau chief for Hearst Newspapers, came calling with an offer to be a columnist, I gratefully said, Why not? After all those years of telling it like it is, now I can tell it how I want it to be. To put another point on it, I get to wake up every morning and say, "Who am I mad at today?"

I also got a call from Lisa Drew at Scribner, who made my book *Front Row at the White House* happen. She suggested I try another, this time a lighter look at all those presidents who have known me. When a friend of mine heard about the project, she said, "Gee, Helen, do you think these are very funny guys?"

"Well," I said, "I told Lisa it might be a pretty thin book."

Not only did I discover that on the whole, "these guys," their families, and their staffs are indeed a pretty funny lot, but given that they were funny while they were in office, I think it could be described as its own genus of humor: *humorata presidentis*—maybe that's what George W. Bush would call it. There also have been the poignant, the touching, and the sad moments in their lives, the kind that have given the public a human touchstone. Some things that have happened could just as well have happened to a member of your family, a neighbor, a coworker; we should remember that presidents are people, too. They just get to live rent-free for four or eight years, travel in their own aircraft, and have someone else pick up the dry cleaning.

Each president I've covered has also displayed his own kind of humor, from Kennedy's wit to George W. Bush's Middle English. Johnson had the down-home story and the stem-winder; Ford had dry observation and a pratfall or two; Reagan had the impeccable anecdote; Bush senior had his own way of "plain speaking" and a dislike for broccoli; Clinton had great timing and was smart enough to joke about how smart he is; Carter had his comebacks; and Nixon—well, I did say it was going to be a pretty thin book.

Humor is a saving grace in the White House. And if a president has a sense of humor—even better, wit—it goes a long way to lighten the atmosphere and to bring people together for a good laugh.

Of the presidents I covered in the White House, John F. Kennedy and Ronald Reagan were the best at deflecting the sometimes bitter acrimony associated with hard-driving politics and at easing the tension. Neither of these two presidents hesitated to use the weapon at their command that gave them an aura of being good-natured and still confident. They had on their side that the public liked—and sometimes adored—them.

But that didn't mean they didn't cuss out their tormentors and have a few choice profane words for those who crossed them. Even Kennedy had to admit at a news conference that he had said, "My father always used to say that businessmen were SOBs." He said that after Roger Blough, president of U.S. Steel, had gone back on a promise not to raise steel prices.

For choice words that are not spoken in public, listen to the tapes of private conversations of Presidents Lyndon B. Johnson and Richard Nixon.

Self-deprecating humor has come into style in recent years with presidents. It is a surefire winner, especially before press audiences such as at the Gridiron Club, the White House Correspondents Association, and the Radio-Television Correspondents Association dinners. If the joke is on the president, all to the good.

It disarms his usual detractors and conveys a sense of good sportsmanship. In other words, anything for a laugh. But, hey, it works and warms up the crowd with a heavy dose of bonhomie.

How does the saying go? Laugh and the world laughs with

you. Cry and you cry alone. In the years I covered the White House, there have probably been more somber, grim times to recall. But the humor has always been appreciated. We in the press have not been immune. We have often been the butt of a joke, probably not repeatable. Some, such as LBJ and Nixon, have called us names. President George W. Bush tags reporters with nicknames.

In his wonderful book *Humor and the Presidency,* Gerald Ford noted there are two ways to become an authority on humor: "The first way is to become one of the perpetrators. You know them: comedians, satirists, cartoonists, and impersonators. The second way to gain such credentials is to be the victim of their merciless talents. As such a victim, I take a back seat to no one as far as humor is concerned."

In the foreword to *Humor and the Presidency,* Edward Bennett Williams wrote: "Humor is indispensable to democracy. It is the ingredient lacking in all the dictatorships in what seems to be an increasingly authoritarian world. It is the element that permits us to laugh at ourselves and with each other, whether we be political friends or foes."

I couldn't agree more.

When I started to look back, remember, and check my files for this book, I was struck by the sheer number of remembrances, anecdotes, news conferences, press briefings, and by the other millions or so words uttered by presidents, first ladies, aides—and the accompanying media accounts—which made for some lively reading. I was also prompted to include events that touched the nation, made us shed a tear, left us breathless or just bewildered. I also recalled events that reminded me of the awesome power and responsibility of the presidency and the personal strength and public travails of some chief executives.

As for September 11, 2001—we look back on September 10 as the end of the good old days, when we were carefree and confident, and we thought we were going to live happily ever after. But our world, and everyone else's, has changed, and we may never return to the America we once knew with our essential liberties intact.

I hope we encounter this brave new world with courage and a fierce intention to keep our freedoms and not lose them all in the name of national security. Benjamin Franklin said if we give up our essential freedoms for some security, we are in danger of losing both.

And when all is said and done, let's hope there will be happy times again, more smiles and more laughter in the twenty-first century.

Helping me put it together was a great network of ex-colleagues at United Press International who shared coverage duties with me at the White House and across the country. They all combed their files and their memories (some didn't have to worry about their hair) and sent me a number of stories for inclusion. I thank them all for their generosity and I've named names. I hope I've done right by them.

So, let's settle back and enjoy. After all, as Samuel Butler remarked, "Man is the only animal with a sense of humor—and a state legislature."

I am often told how lucky I have been to see history in the making in the White House and to observe our leaders in their triumphs and defeats. All I can say is "Thanks for the memories, Mr. President."

JOHN F. KENNEDY

John F. Kennedy was the first president I covered nonstop. He was chummier with the press than any other I have covered because, I think, he was one of us: the first president born in the twentieth century. He knew about our deadlines, our problems, our policies, and our shenanigans. He also knew that reporters satirized members of the handsome Kennedy clan at every opportunity. He was a convenient target with his youthful looks, his accent, his hair, and that finger-jabbing he would do when answering questions. But he took it all in stride and sometimes even enjoyed it. In an interview with college students for Medill News Service in 2001, I said Lyndon B. Johnson was my favorite president to cover but JFK was the president I liked best because of his vision— launching the Peace Corps and promising to put a man on the moon. As I told the students, "Great presidents set great goals for mankind."

As Kennedy rode in an open car through several Massachusetts towns during the 1960 campaign, Catholic nuns would turn out in droves, lining the streets and hailing the candidate. An aide asked Kennedy if he thought the priests would vote for him. "I don't know," he said, "but I'm sure the nuns will."

Two of Kennedy's most formidable opponents in the Democratic primaries were fellow senators, Stuart Symington of Missouri and Senate Majority Leader Lyndon B. Johnson of Texas, who was particularly formidable, given his long legislative service and his huge ambition. Of his two opponents, Kennedy liked to relate the following story:

"I dreamed about the 1960 campaign last night, and I told Stuart Symington and Lyndon Johnson about it in the [Senate] cloakroom yesterday. I told them how the Lord came into my bedroom, anointed my head, and said, 'John Kennedy, I hereby anoint you president of the United States.' Stu Symington said, 'That's strange, Jack, because I, too, had a similar dream last night, in which the Lord anointed me and declared me president of the United States.' And Lyndon Johnson said, 'That's very interesting, gentlemen, because I, too, had a similar dream last night—and I don't remember anointing either one of you.'"

Kennedy's religion was a key campaign issue, but he was able to use humor here as well, in his disarming way. "The reporters are constantly asking me my views of the pope's infallibility," he said. "And so I asked my friend Cardinal Spellman what I should say when reporters ask me whether I feel the pope is infallible. And Cardinal Spellman said, 'I don't know what to tell you, Senator. All I know is that he keeps calling me Spillman.'"

In a speech before the Women's National Press Club, Arthur Larson, former director of the U.S. Information Agency under Eisenhower, suggested that Senator Kennedy switch his party allegiance and become a "new" Republican. This was Mr. Kennedy's reply: "One temptation to accept Mr. Larson's invitation to become a 'new' Republican is the fact that I would be the first senator in either party to do so."

One thing that struck a chord with the public was not only Jackie Kennedy's sense of style but JFK's sartorial flair. But that dress-for-success look was put to the test on the campaign trail one night in Houston when Kennedy was to speak to a group of Presbyterian ministers. In his book *Johnny, We Hardly Knew Ye*, Kenneth O'Donnell recalled Kennedy calling for Dave Powers, who saw to all things for the candidate. It seemed Powers was about to make JFK commit a fashion faux pas because Powers had only packed brown shoes. Kennedy asked O'Donnell if he had any black shoes he could borrow, and O'Donnell said he had no extra black shoes.

"Well, it's too late now," Kennedy muttered. "I ought to send Powers back to Charlestown on this one."

So Kennedy donned the brown shoes and headed for the elevator with his aides. Holding the door was Powers, trying to act as if nothing had happened. JFK stared at Powers, then looked down at his blue suit and brown shoes and looked at Powers again. As the elevator descended, Powers stared off into space.

"Dave, do you notice anything out of place in my attire?" Kennedy asked.

Powers cleared his throat nervously and said, "Are those brown shoes?"

"Yes," said Kennedy. "These are brown shoes. Brown shoes with a dark blue suit. Thanks very much, Dave."

"Well, Senator," said Powers, "they won't see your shoes on television. Besides, you know most the men in this country wear brown shoes. Do you realize tonight, by wearing these shoes, you'll be sewing up the brown-shoe voters?"

Kennedy laughed and went off to face the ministers.

Kennedy's campaign motorcades always drew crowds, and in those crowds were throngs of young women hardly able to contain their enthusiasm for the candidate. The traveling press had nicknames for all of them: the *squealers,* the *jumpers,* the *runners,* the *leapers,* and the *criers.*

As for presidential news conferences, in my experience JFK and Bill Clinton would probably rank at the top when it comes to quick wit and ready repartee. JFK actually seemed to enjoy sparring with members of the press. We got the first inklings of what we would be in for at the White House during the 1960 presidential campaign. Just as candidates do now, he spoke at innumerable fund-raising dinners, and one October night, in Green Bay, Wisconsin, he told the crowd, "Ladies and gentlemen, I was warned to be out in plenty of time to permit those who are going to the Green Bay Packers game to leave. I don't mind running against Mr. Nixon, but I have the good sense not to run against the Green Bay Packers."

One of the more popular stories that circulated during the 1960 campaign was when Kennedy visited a mine in West Virginia.

"Is it true you're the son of one of our wealthiest men?" asked one of the miners.

Kennedy admitted that this was true.

"Is it true you've never wanted for anything and had everything you wanted?"

"I guess so," said Kennedy.

"Is it true you've never done a day's work with your hands all your life?"

At this Kennedy nodded.

"Well, let me tell you this," said the miner. "You haven't missed a thing."

At another speech in New York City, Kennedy commented on the debt the Democratic Party was accumulating with the campaign: "I have been informed that with this dinner I am now responsible as the leader of the Democratic Party for a debt of over one million dollars. I don't know—they spend it like they were sure we were going to win."

The Republicans used Kennedy's lack of experience as an issue in the 1960 presidential campaign. At a speech in Minneapolis a month before the election, Kennedy told the crowd, "Ladies and gentlemen, the outstanding news story of this week was not the events of the United Nations or even the presidential campaign. It was the story coming out of my own city of Boston that Ted Williams of the Boston Red Sox had retired from baseball. It seems that at forty-two he was too old. It shows that perhaps experience isn't enough."

Religion was a big issue in the Kennedy-Nixon race, and the future president handled the question delicately but forcefully.

During the 1960 primary campaign in Morgantown, West Virginia, he decided to meet the religious issue head-on, and after speaking of the need for change in government, he told a street crowd, "Nobody asked me if I was a Catholic when I joined the United States Navy."

He went on in a passionate vein and asked if 40 million Americans lost their right to run for the presidency on the day when they were baptized as Catholics.

"That wasn't the country my brother died for in Europe," he said. "And nobody asked my brother if he was a Catholic or a Protestant before he climbed into an American bomber plane to fly his last mission."

At an appearance before a meeting of Presbyterian ministers in Houston, Kennedy told them, "Because I am a Catholic and no Catholic has ever been elected president, the real issues in this campaign have been obscured. So it is apparently necessary for me to state again not what kind of church I believe in, for that should be important only to me, but what kind of America I believe in. I believe in an America where the separation of the church and state is absolute, where no Catholic prelate would tell the president how to act and no Presbyterian minister would tell his parishioners for whom to vote . . . where no man is denied public office merely because his religion differs from the president who might appoint him or the people who might elect him."

JFK knew his poetry. On the campaign trail in 1960 he ended a speech at New York University quoting his favorite poet, Robert Frost, saying, "But I have promises to keep . . . and miles to go before I sleep . . . and miles to go before I sleep."

He paused and then added: "And now I go to Brooklyn."

My boss in the White House bureau at UPI when I first started was the great Merriman Smith. Smitty, as he was known, was one of the most tenacious, fearless reporters I'd ever worked with, his prodigious output of stories matched only by that of his AP counterpart, my husband, Douglas Cornell. On election night in 1960, Smitty was dispatched to Massachusetts, and upon seeing him, Kennedy remarked, "Does this mean I've won?"

Elected at the age of forty-three, Kennedy was often asked what he would do when he left the White House since he would be younger than most of his predecessors. His reply: "I'll be too young to write my memoirs and too old to start a new career."

Kennedy always went out of his way to recognize Johnson's sensitivity and not to ruffle his feelings, although his brother Bobby detested LBJ and vice versa. In *Johnny, We Hardly Knew Ye,* Kenneth O'Donnell and Dave Powers recalled that on election night in 1960, Johnson phoned from his ranch to say Texas was very close, but safe, and also told Kennedy, "I see we won in Pennsylvania, but what happened to you in Ohio?"

Kennedy definitely wanted his brother Bobby to be in the cabinet as attorney general, but there was the question of nepotism. It was humorously considered that Kennedy would come out on his porch in fashionable Georgetown in the dead of night and whisper, "It's Bobby." When the announcement occurred during the Christmas season, Bobby flew to Palm Beach, Florida, to join his family. We reporters also went to the West Palm Beach airport, and when Ethel Kennedy saw her husband, Bobby, at the top of the stairs, she flashed a big smile and shouted, "We did it."

There was less criticism than expected.

At a press conference in Anchorage, Alaska, in September 1960, a reporter asked, "Senator, you were promised [a] military intelligence briefing from the president. Have you received that?"

"Yes," said Kennedy, "I talked on Thursday morning to General Wheeler from the Defense Department."

"What was his first name?" the reporter asked.

"He didn't brief me on that," said Kennedy.

Early in his term, a reporter asked Kennedy, "If you had to do it over again, would you work for the presidency and would you recommend the job to others?"

"Well," said JFK, "the answer to the first is yes, and the answer to the second is no. I don't recommend it to others, at least not for a while."

Kennedy's news conferences always had a good deal of back-and-forth; he enjoyed bantering with the press. I remember the venerable May Craig got up and, in her combined Southern-and-Maine twang, asked Kennedy what he had done for women lately. "Well, obviously, Mrs. Craig," he said, "not enough."

At his meeting with Soviet leader Nikita Khrushchev in Vienna, the president noticed a medal on Khrushchev's chest and asked what it was. Khrushchev replied that it was the Lenin Peace Prize.

"I hope you keep it," Kennedy commented.

* * *

So many times I heard Kennedy say the Chinese proverb "A journey of a thousand miles begins with the first step."

In his meeting with Khrushchev, the Soviet leader also commented, "You seem to know the Chinese well."

To which Kennedy responded prophetically, "We may both get to know them better."

Jackie Kennedy, however, was a whole other matter when it came to coverage. At thirty-one, she didn't seem too enthusiastic about the nonstop coverage, and as a mother of two small children, she was fiercely protective of their privacy. In early 1960, someone asked her where she thought the Democratic National Convention should be held. "Acapulco," she replied.

On the campaign trail, coverage of Jackie's clothes, hairstyle, and fashion sense netted quite a bit of attention. At one point, rather annoyed, she told Nan Robertson of the *New York Times* that if all the reports about her spending habits were true, "I'd be wearing sable underwear."

In March 1961, Congress honored the poet Robert Frost, presenting him with a Congressional Medal recognizing his achievements and contributions to American letters. At the White House ceremony to present Frost with the medal, Kennedy noted that perhaps Frost was disappointed because not only had the vote been a noncontroversial issue, it had been unanimous: "It's the only thing they've been able to agree on for a long time."

In *The Wit and Wisdom of John F. Kennedy,* edited by Alex Ayres, it was noted that the Kennedys hosted many dinners for artists at the White House.

"It's become a sort of eating place for artists," Kennedy was heard to say. "But they never ask us out."

* * *

At a White House dinner honoring Nobel Prize winners, among the guests was theoretical chemist and Nobel winner Linus Pauling, who had spent the day picketing the White House in a ban-the-bomb protest. After the demonstration, Pauling went to his hotel, changed into a tuxedo, and returned to the White House for dinner, whereupon Kennedy greeted him with an appropriate sally: "I'm glad you decided to come inside to dinner."

Jacqueline Kennedy was an extremely shy and private person but the public loved her, and she became renowned for her glamour and sense of mystique. She could also be tough. Once when a naval aide annoyed her, she told him in no uncertain terms, "Shape up or ship out."

In Columbus, Ohio, in 1961, Kennedy said, "I do not want it said of our generation what T. S. Eliot wrote in 'The Rock': 'And the wind will say these were decent people. Their only monument an asphalt road and a thousand lost golf balls.'

"We can do better than that."

Long before women were admitted to the National Press Club, there was the Women's National Press Club, and we staged a show every year, lampooning the high and the mighty with song and dance. In December 1961, I got to portray Jackie in a song written by Sidney Schwartz and Gwen Gibson that went:

> If I want to fly away
> Without taking JFK
> That's me, Jackie.

> If I'm fond of French champagne
> If I'd rather not campaign
> That's me, Jackie.

If I want to give a ball
For just me and Charles de Gaulle
I have abso-lutely all the gall
I need . . .

If I like to water-ski
And I want my private sea
Don't look askance,
With half the chance,
You'd be like me, Jackie.

Si je suis très débonnaire
Or wear sable underwear
That's me—Jackie.

If I like to live in style
On my own Aegean isle
That's me, Jackie.

If I use Mount Vernon's lawn
For amusing Ayub Khan
And we choose to dance till dawn
Then *c'est la vie.*

If I rewrite history
Name the White House "Chez Jackie,"
Am I to blame?
You'd do the same
If you were me—Jackie.

Pierre Salinger, JFK's hardworking press secretary, was used to getting strange calls at strange hours from reporters and recalled, "Helen Thomas of UPI woke me out of a sound sleep one morning at three o'clock. 'I wouldn't call you at an ungodly hour like this, Pierre, if it weren't important. But we have a report that one of Caroline's hamsters has died. Would you check it out for me?'

"I exploded. 'Who would you like me to call, Helen? Caroline? Mrs. Kennedy? The president himself?' I fell back into bed without waiting for her answer.

"Later that morning, I found out that Helen was correct. One of Caroline's hamsters had, indeed, crawled into the president's bathtub and drowned."

In 1961 women reporters in Washington were waging an uphill battle to be allowed to cover major speeches by local and visiting dignitaries at the all-male National Press Club. Women were allowed to listen to the newsmakers but were not permitted to eat there and had to sit in the balcony, watching their male counterparts dine in comfort below. As president of the Women's National Press Club, I had sent cables to a number of heads of state, including Nikita Khrushchev, urging them to speak at our club instead of the National Press Club, on grounds that we provided a balanced and integrated audience.

Venezuela's President Rómulo Betancourt had also been apprised of the matter, but he spoke at the National Press Club anyway, then went to the White House for a meeting with JFK. When the meeting ended, JFK escorted his guest through the lobby of the West Wing. A number of reporters stopped the two and asked for a comment.

"I just told the National Press Club that I felt it might be a good idea to permit women correspondents to join their club activities," Betancourt said.

"There's one of your revolutionaries right over there," said Kennedy, pointing to me. "Here she is trying to bring her own revolt into the White House."

Over the laughter, I told Betancourt, "We forgive you, officially."

"But not personally," said Kennedy.

* * *

The "space race" with the Soviet Union hit a high note in the spring of 1961, when astronaut Alan Shephard Jr. made the first successful space flight for the Americans. In a ceremony honoring him, Kennedy's laudatory remarks were to the point, as were his words on what might have happened if the test had not gone as planned:

"We have with us today the nation's number one television performer, who I think on last Friday morning secured the largest rating of any morning show in recent history. And I think it does credit to him that he is associated with such a distinguished group of Americans whom we are all glad to honor today—his companions in the flight to outer space—so I think I'll give them all a hand. They are the tanned and healthy ones—the rest are Washington employees.

"I also want to pay a particular tribute to some of the people who worked in this flight: Robert Gilruth, who was director of the Space Task Force Group at Langley Field; Walter Williams, the operations director of Project Mercury; the NASA deputy administrator, Dr. Hugh Dryden; Lieutenant Colonel John Glenn Jr.; and of course, Jim Webb, who is head of NASA.

"Most of these names are unfamiliar. If the flight had not been an overwhelming success, these names would be very familiar to everyone."

At his first Gridiron dinner as president in the spring of 1961, Kennedy decided to respond to reports about his brother Bobby's relative inexperience, given his appointment as attorney general.

"Bobby has just received his law degree," JFK told the crowd, "and we thought he should have some experience before he goes into private practice."

I've said time and time again that no president has ever liked the press, and these days I still stand by that assessment. But each one in his own way has recognized the necessity of the job of covering the White House. While Kennedy said of the nation's newspapers after he was in office—and after the press began covering him seven days a week, twenty-four hours a day—"I'm reading more and enjoying it less," he did pay tribute to those in the press corps and the value of the media at large when he spoke to the American Society of Newspaper Editors in April 1961:

"I appreciate very much your generous invitation to be here tonight.

"You bear heavy responsibilities these days, and an article I read some time ago reminded me of how particularly heavy the burdens of present-day events bear upon your profession.

"You may remember that in 1851, the *New York Herald Tribune,* under the sponsorship of Horace Greeley, included as its London correspondent an obscure journalist by the name of Karl Marx.

"We are told that the foreign correspondent, Marx, stone broke and with a family ill and undernourished, constantly appealed to Greeley and managing editor Charles Dana for an increase in his munificent salary of five dollars per installment, a salary which he and Engels labeled as 'the lousiest petty bourgeois cheating.'

"But when all his financial appeals were refused, Marx looked around for other means of livelihood and fame and eventually terminated his relationship with the *Tribune* and devoted his talents full-time to the cause that would bequeath to the world the seeds of Leninism, Stalinism, revolution, and the Cold War.

"If only this capitalistic New York newspaper would have treated him more kindly, if only Marx had remained a foreign correspondent, history might have been different, and I hope all publishers will bear this lesson in mind the next time they receive a poverty-stricken appeal for a small increase in the expense account from an obscure newspaperman.

"I have selected as the title of my remarks tonight 'The President and the Press.' Some may suggest that this would be more naturally worded 'The President *vs.* the Press,' but those are not my sentiments tonight.

"It is true, however, that when a well-known diplomat from another country demanded recently that our State Department repudiate certain newspaper attacks on his colleague, it was necessary for us to reply that this administration was not responsible for the press, for the press had already made it clear that it was not responsible for this administration.

"If in the last few months your White House reporters and photographers have been attending church services with regularity, that has surely done them no harm.

"On the other hand, I realize that your staff and wire service photographers may be complaining that they do not enjoy the same green privileges at the local golf courses which they once did. It is true that my predecessor did not object as I do to pictures of one's golfing skill in action. But neither, on the other hand, did he ever bean a Secret Service man."

UPI held a dinner for Kennedy on June 9, 1961. In his speech, he noted that he had worked for a time for International News Service, the *I* that got attached to *United Press* when the two companies merged. "I used to work for INS for a short time," he said, "although I never have been able to figure out whether UP belongs to INS or INS belongs to UP."

Then he noted the omnipresence of Smitty at the White House, saying, "I want to say that I come here not as a stranger, because I have had in my first months in office the close observation of Mr. Merriman Smith, who carried other presidents through difficult periods before, and who is regarded as one of the leading presidential collectors of our time."

The Kennedys were returning from a trip to Hyannis Port one weekend, and Joseph P. Kennedy had given Jackie a German shepherd puppy that she named Clipper. The press corps sent a note to the family quarters in the front of the plane and asked her what she planned on feeding the newest addition to the Kennedy pets. She wrote back, "Reporters."

Her children, however, were a source of delight—when we were able to see and talk to them. One day, we spotted Caroline, then three, wandering around. "Where's your daddy?" someone asked her. She replied, "He's upstairs with his shoes and socks off, doing nothing."

"Helen would be a nice girl if she'd ever get rid of that pad and pencil," Kennedy told Salinger in the early days of the administration. On one occasion, Salinger called reporters and photographers to the Oval Office for a picture-taking session.

I was the only member of the writing press in the lobby at the time, so off I went, the lone "pad and pencil" reporter amid all the cameramen.

Kennedy looked up, assessed those assembled, and said, "Well, if it isn't Miss Thomas of the Universal Press."

I usually drew press duty on Sundays with Kennedy, which meant accompanying him to church. He would take Communion in private and seemed a bit embarrassed about being observed as a devout, practicing Catholic, feeling no doubt a spiritual display was not his style.

One day the press filed into the Oval Office for a picture-taking session, and Kennedy asked me whether I was going on his upcoming trip to New York.

"No, Mr. President," I said, "I only go to church with you."

A few days later, I was standing behind the rope, doing the usual press checkout, and as he boarded the helicopter, he spotted me and grinned. "You get all the good trips," he said.

* * *

Following Jackie to church was another story. She had dubbed me and Fran Lewine of Associated Press "the harpies" and was constantly complaining that we wouldn't leave her alone. One day she summoned the Secret Service agents and told them "two strange-looking Spanish women" were following her.

I was constantly amazed by Kennedy's grasp. In the middle of a hectic schedule he would notice some minute detail and find humor in it. Just before Jackie had received her $7,000 Somali leopard coat from Emperor Haile Selassie, I had bought a fake leopard number of my own, on sale for $40. One chilly autumn day, I wore my bargain coat to cover Kennedy's helicopter arrival on the Ellipse. I was standing amid a number of reporters, photographers, aides, and tourists when he stepped off the chopper, spotted me, and yelled over the crowd, "Everybody's wearing leopard these days!"

On St. Patrick's Day in 1962, the White House hosted a party for a number of friends and family members. I walked up to JFK and he started talking about Caroline, noting that she had thought up the name Leprechaun for her new pony, given to her by Ireland's President Eamon de Valera.

"It's a great day for the Irish," I said.

"So what are you doing here?" he quipped.

In 1962 I covered Kennedy's working luncheon with German Chancellor Konrad Adenauer. In a toast, the chancellor said his visit had been beneficial "although we know these communiqués are written in advance."

After the meeting, Kennedy escorted Adenauer to his limousine and I asked Kennedy about the meeting. "You'll be getting a communiqué from me," he said.

"Is that the one you wrote before he came?" I asked.

* * *

Al Neuharth, the man who delivered *USA Today* to the nation, has had a long and illustrious career in the newspaper business. He now lives near Cape Canaveral, Florida, and told a story that he gleaned from the astronauts in training at the Cape. It seems that in 1961, Kennedy invited the astronauts of his era to a White House dinner in their honor.

During the conversation, JFK asked them, "Do you think we can land on the moon?"

Not wanting to say anything was impossible to the president of the United States, the astronauts told Kennedy, "Absolutely" and "Yeah, sure—you bet."

When they left the White House, the astronauts turned to each other and said, "Is this guy nuts? Is he crazy?"

Within a year Kennedy announced in a speech to the United Nations that the United States had a goal of putting men on the moon in a decade. He didn't live to see it. But Lyndon B. Johnson kept the vision alive with the necessary funding, and Neil Armstrong landed on the moon in July 1969. He was officially greeted by President Nixon on a ship in the Pacific. And what president's name did the astronauts put on the moon? "President Richard M. Nixon." Such is fate.

In 1961, according to *Wit and Wisdom,* after Kennedy blocked the steel price hike, a gloomy businessman came to call, and he was reassured by an upbeat president.

"Things look great," Kennedy told his caller. "Why, if I weren't president, I'd be buying stock."

"If you weren't president, so would I," the businessman replied.

I became the first woman to close a presidential news conference, but looking back, I think my first attempt was without much aplomb. Merriman Smith, who traditionally closed them with his loud "Thank you, Mr. President," was out of town. I closely watched the clock during the session, and at what I thought was the appropriate time, I stood up and said my line—"Thank you, Mr. President"—but got drowned out by a chorus of newsmen still seeking recognition. It was a terrifying moment. I waited a bit longer until Kennedy was struggling with the answer to a complicated question and shouted, "Thank you, Mr. President!"

Kennedy looked over and said, "Thank *you,* Helen."

After another news conference I spotted Kennedy standing at a side entrance to the White House, puffing on a cigar and looking pretty satisfied with himself.

"Boy, you really handled that one," I said, and added I was quite impressed with how he had reeled off some esoteric statistics about the number of gallons of molasses that went into daily Cuban sugar production.

Kennedy laughed and said, "Someone came in and gave me the figures a few hours before the conference."

It may be hard to believe in these post–Cold War times that the Cuban missile crisis nearly brought the United States to war with the Soviet Union. Kennedy agonized over whether to launch a surprise, preemptive strike to destroy the Soviet missiles that had been deployed on the island nation, ninety miles from Florida, or to impose a naval blockade and hope the threat of an invasion would deter the Russians.

As the world held its breath in the autumn of 1962, Kennedy huddled nonstop with his advisers. In one meeting, Air Force Chief of Staff General Curtis LeMay told Kennedy, "You're in a pretty bad fix, Mr. President."

"What did you say?" said Kennedy.

LeMay repeated his remark, and Kennedy coolly replied, "Well, maybe you haven't noticed—you're in it with me."

* * *

The White House press corps was so hungry for news during those cold October days when everyone in Washington waited for the other shoe to drop. One afternoon, Kennedy strolled out of the Cabinet Room and Merriman Smith asked him how things were going. "It's been an interesting day," the president replied. Reporters ran to the telephones with that noncommittal remark. It was the lead of the day—even though no one knew what it meant. After all was said and done, I thought about another of JFK's favorite phrases, one I'd heard him say often: "Victory has a thousand fathers; defeat is an orphan."

When he was campaigning for the presidency in 1964, LBJ shared his recollection of the Cuban missile crisis at many a campaign stop. He would tell the crowds: "I sat in the Cabinet Room for thirty-seven meetings during the Cuban missile crisis. I saw Mr. Khrushchev bring his missiles into Cuba, ninety miles from our shores, and point them in our direction. I saw Mr. Kennedy bring in all the men with the stars on their shoulders and the gold braid on their uniforms. I never knew a single morning when I left home that I would see my wife and daughters again that night. It looked like it was just about the time, the clock was ticking. And Mr. Kennedy and Mr. Khrushchev were staring at each other eyeball to eyeball, with the knives at each other's sides.

"But I am proud to tell you we were careful and cautious, and deliberate and sober, and sound—and the coolest man in that room was John Fitzgerald Kennedy, your president."

What was going on inside the White House was wild enough, but an incident was going on outside that I suppose could only happen in America. *The Adventures of Rocky and Bullwinkle* was airing at the time. Not only children but adults enjoyed this one-of-a-kind program for its sophisticated yet wacky treatment of the Cold War, as Rocky and Bullwinkle periodically tangled with agents Boris Badenov and Natasha Fatale. One of the show's creators, Jay Ward, had an irrepressible sense of humor, and a handful of the cartoons dealt with a small island called Moosylvania. Ward had actually bought a small island on a lake in Minnesota, which he named Moosylvania, and then set up a petition drive and nationwide tour to give Moosylvania statehood—"the Only State in the Union with an Entirely Non-Resident Population."

In a PBS interview for the documentary *Of Moose and Men,* Howard Brand, the publicist for the cartoon show, described one series of incredible events:

"We got this van, this poor van with this calliope that played circus music, and we took off cross-country and we visited fifty, sixty cities. . . . It culminated when we got to Washington, D.C., and Jay had this huge list of names—signatures—for statehood for Moosylvania. And we got into the van, and we were accompanied by Pat Humphrey, who was Hubert Humphrey's daughter-in-law, and who was the NBC representative. Jay was driving the van. She was next to him and I was sitting in the back—hiding in the back is more like it—and we got to the White House gate, and the [entrance guard] said, 'What are you doing? . . . Turn off that music!'

"And Jay said, 'We're here to see President Kennedy. We want statehood for Moosylvania.'

"And the guy said, 'Turn around and get out of here!'

"And Jay said, 'You know, you could be civil. I mean—'

"I said, 'Jay, turn around!'

" 'No,' said Jay. 'I don't like his attitude.'

"Of course the guy then started to unbuckle his revolver. And I panicked. 'Jay, let's get out of here!'

" 'Well, I will, but I mean the man is absolutely rude,' said Jay. And we turned around and left."

That afternoon, Brand took the photographs that were taken

of us by the White House and went to the [Associated Press] office.

"Look," he told them, "we tried to get into the White House and they wouldn't let us! I thought Kennedy had a sense of humor."

One of the reporters took him aside and said, "Come over here, let me show you something."

"And he took me over," said Brand, "and showed me the photographs of the Russian ships with the missiles going toward Cuba. . . . We had arrived at the White House on the day of the Cuban missile crisis.

"So nobody paid any attention to us, even though we were very funny.

"That ended the tour, and we drove back home. Never did get statehood for Moosylvania, either."

During his campaign, JFK had pledged to get America moving again. At a press conference in July 1963, a reporter asked him, "Do you think it is moving? And if so, where? The reason I ask you this question, Mr. President, is that the Republican National Committee recently adopted a resolution saying you are pretty much a failure."

"I'm sure it was passed unanimously," Kennedy responded.

For grace and style, I witnessed Kennedy at his best when civil rights leader Martin Luther King came to the White House for a reception soon after he had delivered his famous "I have a dream" speech at the Lincoln Memorial on August 28, 1963.

As King went through the receiving line, Kennedy shook his hand and with a big smile said, "I have a dream."

The Kennedys' trip to Paris is notable for JFK's often-remembered remark: "I'm the man who accompanied Jacqueline Kennedy to Paris."

* * *

Wit and Wisdom recounts another remark when JFK posed for pictures with his host, President Charles de Gaulle. The French president dismissed the photographers with a flick of a finger.

"Don't you wish you could dismiss photographers like that?" a reporter asked Kennedy.

"You must remember," said Kennedy, "I was not recalled to office as my country's savior."

In March 1963, White House reporters were getting a bit annoyed at some of the news management in play. One of the sillier moments occurred when Al Spivak of UPI and another reporter smelled smoke. They asked what was going on and were told a fire extinguisher had been carried "in one hell of a hurry" from the lobby to the "off-limits-to-newsmen" office area.

White House aide Malcolm Kilduff treated the matter rather lightly, telling Al that it was nothing more than someone forgetting to open the damper in the president's fireplace and then lighting a fire. "He denied up and down—to me but not to the AP—that any fire extinguisher had been brought in," said a memo Al later wrote recounting the event. "I took him at his word and found out this morning he had misled me about the fire extinguisher. I also was somewhat miffed at his sneering attitude about, 'Are you guys so hard up you can't find anything else to write about?' so I penned the following note to him:

" 'Thanks for all your help on the fire story, which my opposition got on page one of the *Washington Post* by forgetting to check with you for accuracy. It's an insignificant matter, as you say. People haven't been interested in fires at the White House—particularly in the president's office—since 1814. Andy Tully once wrote a scholarly book called *The Burning of the White House*—but I understand he got his information from a previous administration.' "

* * *

Another item in what Al referred to as "keeping our files up-to-date on the efficacy of White House news handling" came from me in April 1963:

"Picking up the *Washington Post* this morning like any other housewife, I flipped when I saw the story that the Kennedys were seeking a tenant for Rattlesnake Mountain. I got to the White House at 9 A.M., didn't take my coat off, and hit the phone and asked for Pam Turnure. She wasn't in, so I went in to see Kilduff, who said he didn't know but added, 'That makes sense, since they won't be here this summer.' He said he'd check with Pam.

"A couple hours later, still with no answer, I went to [White House aide Andy] Hatcher, who looked at me in astonishment and said, 'Absolutely untrue.' 'May I quote you,' I said. 'No,' he replied, 'we don't want to say anything about it. You check with Pam.' When I called Pam, she apparently was on the line with Mrs. Kennedy. I insisted on waiting with Pam's secretary. I told the secretary that the question was about the house and that Hatcher had denied the story. When Pam got on, her voice was very nervous and she was noticeably disturbed. She referred me back to Hatcher, who would 'correct' what he had told me earlier. I told her, 'Pam, I'm now putting the question to you.' After going back and forth that way a couple times, she said, 'The house is rented. But you go to Hatcher.' I told her I would do that but now I wanted the details, to whom it was rented, etc. She said there would be none at this time. As I was dictating, Hatcher came to the phone booth and said the story was 'true.'

"Also, I forgot to mention that Hatcher told me he had told a reporter yesterday who had queried him that the story was 'ridiculous.'"

The late Aline Mosby, who had a long and legendary career at UPI, accidentally figured in the story of John F. Kennedy's assassination by Lee Harvey Oswald.

Oswald had gone to Russia and tried to renounce his American citizenship. One day Aline, making her beat calls, asked the U.S. consulate in Moscow if there were any newsworthy visitors. She was told that there was nobody important, but an American had walked in and turned in his passport, saying he didn't want it anymore.

Aline called Oswald at the Metropole Hotel and set up an interview. The story didn't amount to much, but Mosby remembered and resurrected it after the assassination of JFK.

I traveled with Kennedy when he attended services at Arlington National Cemetery on Veterans Day, November 11, 1963. He took his young son with him. Kennedy appeared pensive and alone on that sad anniversary. After a while, he realized his son was not in the amphitheater where the ceremonies were being held, and I heard him tell a Secret Service agent, "Go get John-John. I think he'll be lonely out there."

Two weeks later JFK was buried on a gentle hill at Arlington, surrounded by thousands of other slain veterans, near the Custis-Lee mansion.

The late, great reporter Tad Szulc recounted a story long after the Bay of Pigs invasion:

Twenty-three years later, Castro said in twelve hours of interviews with Szulc that he had received a private message from Kennedy the day the president was assassinated seeking a dialogue between their countries.

The Cuban leader also absolved Kennedy of blame for the invasion and said he regarded the president's death as "a terrible blow" for relations between Cuba and the United States, according to Szulc's account, which appeared in *Parade* magazine in 1984.

Castro told him the message was delivered to Havana on November 22, 1963, by Jean Daniel, a French editor. "It was noon," Castro said, "and we were just talking about it when we were informed of the assassination."

After Jackie Kennedy left the White House, she and her children went into seclusion. One can only imagine what her first Christmas without her husband was like. She spent some time in Florida, and UPI's Tony Heffernan shared this story with me about what must have been a trying time:

"In December 1963, I was working as the bureau manager in Mobile, Alabama, and H. L. Stevenson, the Southern division news manager, phoned me to ask if I would take the Jackie assignment, since Helen and Smitty were with LBJ. It was, I guess, because I was the only bachelor and therefore I guess Steve figured I wouldn't mind working on Christmas Day if the story were commensurate with the sacrifice.

"Jackie wasn't cooperating and no one could blame her. For several days we [the press corps] were chasing all over Palm Beach, West Palm Beach, for a glimpse of her, but we never caught up with her. Whenever she would leave the Kennedy compound, she'd exit and quickly slip into a car and be driven away. Our cars were parked too far away to give chase without causing a scene, and under the circumstances that would have been highly inappropriate.

"After a couple of days of coming up with very little, I and our excellent photographer—a stringer whose name I regret that I cannot recall—asked the head of the Secret Service detail to let us get some good photos of her and then we'd leave her alone for good. He said he'd see what he could do.

"The Service tipped us when Jackie would make her next trip to town for some Christmas shopping. At the appointed time, Jackie quickly exited the compound, immediately ducked low, and went quickly to the car door nearest her—and oops, it was locked.

"She was no dummy and immediately she showed she knew what was going on. Jackie quickly stood up straight, head held high, turned toward us, and circled the car to get to the unlocked door on the other side of the vehicle. Our photographer must have gotten off about fifteen frames.

"About one hundred people had been waiting across the street, and they broke into applause. Jackie smiled slightly.

"This was one of those times that I learned that pictures do lie. Jackie was one of the most beautiful people I'd ever seen, but her facial features were angular, and in many of our prints her face resembled the caricature of a witch. I picked out five prints in which she looked fine and [the photo department] asked for us to transmit all five. The freelance photographer was ecstatic because he was making twenty-five dollars per transmitted photo, a fortune in those days. He phoned up his girlfriend, and they took me out to a fine dinner.

"We killed the AP in the play on the Jackie story, which Helen noted from our log, and she relayed that to my father, Pat Heffernan, White House correspondent for Reuters, who was very proud. I never did thank Helen for her kindness—and I do now."

LYNDON B. JOHNSON

I made a common mistake among reporters and chief executives: paying inadequate attention to vice presidents. Yet I have witnessed three successions of vice presidents to the presidency: Harry Truman on the death of Franklin Roosevelt, Lyndon B. Johnson after Kennedy was assassinated, and Gerald Ford after Richard Nixon resigned. We all should realize by now that vice presidents are to be taken seriously. Most of them.

At the 1960 presidential convention, Kennedy offered LBJ the number two spot on the ticket, and Johnson told reporters later, "I wanted to be vice president about as much as I wanted to be pope of Rome."

In the Johnson suite at the Hilton Hotel in Los Angeles, LBJ's Texas friends were divided over whether he should join the ticket. Johnson recalled later, "Senators came in begging, 'Please don't run.' One said, 'If you run, I'm going to shoot you between the eyes.'"

That same person, LBJ noted, then came round again and said, "If you *don't* run, I'm going to shoot you between the eyes."

Johnson asked him what had happened to make the man change his mind, and he told LBJ, "I'm running for election," and thought Johnson being on the ticket would help him.

House Speaker Sam Rayburn finally argued Johnson into going on the ticket.

"How can you say that when at two A.M. you told me not to?" Johnson asked.

"Because I'm a much smarter and wiser man today," Rayburn answered.

After he made his decision, Johnson told reporters, "All my delegation cried. A good many wouldn't speak to me. Friends came in tears and said, 'Don't do this. How can you?' "

But once he assumed the presidency, there was no stopping him. He set out to be the "can-do president" and accomplished much. He had a vast intellect, a knowledge of people, and the instincts of a riverboat gambler. The consummate politician, he liked to say, "I seldom think of politics more than eighteen hours a day."

And while he never made any secret of his delight at being president and his desire to spend four years there as the elected choice of the people, he once referred to the White House grounds as "lonely acres that are surrounded by a big black iron fence."

He had no peer as a storyteller—with the bark turned off, of course. He was earthy and well-known for his barnyard epithets—but his humor always had a point of truth he wanted to drive home.

He had what I guess you could call "rancher's eyes" and a genuine affinity for people—and their vulnerabilities. He enjoyed mimicking friends, colleagues, and enemies. But when he pushed too far, he sometimes—not always—had some remorse.

He seemed to have total recall and was best when he was reminiscing about growing up in his beloved Texas hill country.

He twitted his staff unmercifully, and they were often the butt of his jokes. And he expected them to understand. Surprisingly, most of them did.

If you have ever heard a story about LBJ that seems astounding, unreal, or just too over-the-top, believe me, it's probably true—and then some. Because if I heard the story once from

Johnson, I heard it a dozen times. He used to tell us his father would come into his room at five o'clock in the morning, tweak his toes, and shout, "Get up, Lyndon. Every other boy in town has a head start on you."

When JFK offered Johnson the post of vice president on the Democratic ticket in 1960, LBJ had a tough time convincing his wife, Lady Bird, and the Texas delegation that he should take Kennedy's offer. Lady Bird and the other Texans felt they had been slighted, ignored, and humiliated. But Johnson's convincing argument to his wife was "Don't you know I'll be one heartbeat away from the presidency?"

Johnson could orate for hours on end, a combination statesman, evangelist, and medicine man. At a speech in Eufaula, Oklahoma, he told the crowd, "If any of you have martyr complexes, you are going to be disappointed. If any of you are distressed and depressed with yourself and expect me to come down here and feel sorry for you, you are going to be disappointed. Some of our friends talk about a crisis a week. Well, sometimes I don't think they know much about the government until we have a crisis a day and a crisis an hour. And we're always having crises. But we're not going to be crybabies. We're going to stand up like men and face them and we're going to win."

Leonard Marks, a great Washington communications lawyer who was well versed in FCC applications and broadcast cases, was also Lyndon B. Johnson's lawyer. Johnson was Senate majority leader at the time, and he and Lady Bird had purchased a radio station in Austin, Texas, with her money, an inheritance of some $60,000 from her father. It was in the 1950s and Marks had been trying to persuade the couple to put in their bid for a black-and-white television channel in Austin. At breakfast one day, Marks pointed out that they were nearing a deadline on applying for a TV channel. Johnson had been talking to the television moguls in New York, and they had urged him to wait for color television.

"I told you no several times," an irked Johnson told Marks.

At which point, Lady Bird Johnson piped up, gently but clearly, and said, "Lyndon, it's *my* money and I want to do it."

They bought the channel and kept a lucrative television monopoly in Austin for years until the competition moved in.

Johnson suffered a heart attack in 1955 while he was in the Senate. At the time he had ordered two custom-made suits, one blue and one brown. After he was stricken, aides came to him and asked what he wanted them to tell the tailor. He said, "Tell him to go ahead with the suits. I'll need the blue one, in any case."

When the Johnsons moved into the White House, Lady Bird told reporters that she "walked on tiptoe and talked in a whisper." Following Jackie's tenure there would not be easy. But the day Jackie left the White House, she left a small bouquet and a note addressed to Lady Bird, who was touched by Jackie's kindness and consideration after those devastating days.

"I wish you a happy arrival in your new house, Lady Bird," said the note. "Remember—you will be happy here."

Johnson himself never made any bones about his unhappiness with being vice president. One day a reporter asked Lady Bird how she made the best of the situation. She replied, "At least we get our pictures in the papers."

Despite his large and fragile ego, LBJ could poke fun at himself now and then, even though self-deprecating humor was not a big part of his arsenal. At a speech one night, he got a glowing introduction and began his remarks by saying, "I wish my mother and father could have heard that. My father would enjoy it and my mother would believe it."

The Johnsonisms never ceased to strain our credulity. When he became president, he told UPI's great White House reporter Merriman Smith and others, "There's no reason why members of the White House press corps shouldn't be the best-informed, most-respected, and highest-paid reporters in Washington. If you help me, I'll help you. I'll make you big men in your profession."

The remark was no big deal, of course—reporters don't play that way. The strange part was, Smitty was already a big man in his profession—he'd won a Pulitzer Prize. And both he and another "big man" in the profession—my late husband, Doug Cornell, who had covered the White House for AP—knew that they would be writing stories in the future that would make Johnson hit the ceiling.

One of those stories resulted when Doug observed the president picking up one of his beagles, Him, by the ears. Johnson's behavior evoked howls from dog lovers and caused protests from humane societies. Johnson explained, "If you ever follow dogs, you like to hear them yelp. It does them good to let them bark." And that made the situation even more touchy. It was Doug who ended up in the doghouse for a while—we all did, sooner or later.

In his memoir *Lyndon B. Johnson,* press secretary George Reedy wrote that some journalists in Washington greatly admired Johnson as a political master. But Reedy said they hesitated to write anything nice for fear of being considered "trained seals." One reporter who admired Johnson very much was Phil Potter of the *Baltimore Sun.* Johnson called him one day and told him he wanted "a certain story" written. Potter told him to call the advertising department and hung up the phone while LBJ was still talking.

Reporters weren't the only ones to feel the wrath of Johnson—his press secretaries more often than not bore their share when the boss was displeased.

Once while at the Texas ranch, he telephoned George Reedy, who was staying at the guesthouse, a stone's throw away. A friend in the Johnsons' living room heard LBJ read Reedy the riot act and lace his tirade with abusive profanity.

When LBJ finished and hung up, he turned to the friend and said, "Now, let's go give him his birthday gift."

The friend was incredulous, telling Johnson he had overheard him rake Reedy over the coals and asking him how he could even think of giving Reedy a gift after that kind of explosion.

"That's when you give a gift," said Johnson, and the two drove a shiny, new white station wagon over to the guesthouse for Reedy—Johnson's birthday gift to Reedy.

At a bill-signing ceremony in 1963, Johnson made a great show of handing out pens he used to the assembled guests. Handing one to House Speaker John McCormack, he noted, "I found out that if you get along with the Speaker, you get these signing ceremonies more often. I think the Speaker works on the basis that a bill a day keeps the president away."

But those pens were a way of life for Johnson. When he signed the antipoverty bill in August 1964—one of the keystones of his administration—and a bill increasing the powers of the Securities and Exchange Commission, he used 114 pens to write his name twice, once on the $947.5 million legislation and once on the SEC bill. For the antipoverty bill, he dipped seventy-two pens in ink and began a fifteen-minute process of placing dots, curlicues, and little lines on paper. Put all together, they spelled Lyndon B. Johnson. The point was for LBJ to hand a pen to each member of Congress, cabinet member, labor leader, or any other distinguished guest on hand for the ceremony.

For the SEC bill he used forty-two pens the same way.

The White House said it had lost track of how many pens Johnson had used in the first nine months he'd been in office. But in keeping with his talent for multitasking, he was able, when the crowd was unusually large, not only to keep track of how many times he had signed his name and the number of pens needed, but also to keep the line moving. "I don't want any of you all to miss any votes on the Hill," he would tell lawmakers.

There were reports that the pens were donated to the White House, but an aide said they were paid for out of LBJ's personal funds and retailed for about $1. His propensity for handing out pens differed from his early days in office. In December 1963, he was new on the job and had thirty-six pens in front of him to sign a bill providing federal funds to states and local communities to combat air pollution. He handed out thirty-two to congressmen present and commented about looking into the bidding of government contracts for pens "in order not to increase the federal budget." With that, he carefully pocketed the remaining four pens for later use.

The Johnsons had a wonderful black cook, Zephyr Wright, who was considered a part of the family. One day at LBJ's home in Washington while he was still the Senate majority leader, Johnson told Zephyr that he wanted her and her husband, Sammy, to pack up and drive to the LBJ ranch in Texas to prepare for the Johnsons' vacation stay.

"I'm not going to do it," Zephyr told Johnson defiantly. She explained that on the two-day trip, she would have to substitute the bushes on the road for a rest room, brown-bag it from restaurants that would not serve blacks, and her husband would have to sleep in the backseat of the car and she in the front seat below the steering wheel because they could not get into a hotel. Johnson told reporters of her plight many times, and when it came time to sign the Civil Rights Act of 1964, which he had proposed, he gave one of the first pens after the signing to Zephyr Wright.

"You deserve this more than anyone else," Johnson told Wright.

Jokes about LBJ's frugality abounded, especially when it came to keeping everyone in the dark—literally. During the 1964 campaign, he was trying to establish that image and made a great point of turning off all the lights in the White House. As a result, Lady Bird once stumbled in the dark at the foot of a stairway, and White House officers were always bumping into each other. One evening LBJ's aide Joe Laitin left the press office to get a sandwich and—uh-oh—left the light burning in his office. When he returned, a Secret Service agent said to him, "Hey, don't go in there. LBJ is sitting at your desk waiting to find out who left the light on."

"I grabbed a cab and went home," Laitin said later.

As a "public service" in LBJ's presidency, the White House and the Curtis Publishing Co. prepared a new children's book about a "typical American family" that lives in an apartment with fifty-four rooms and sixteen bathrooms. The book was put together to send to youngsters who wrote asking for information about the executive mansion. The president's wife was referred to as "a friendly, unassuming dynamo of activity," and the book revealed that their two daughters, Lynda Bird and Luci Baines, had learned from their parents to be "independent, responsible, and resourceful girls." President Johnson was described as "a friendly man, active, quick-thinking, fast-moving; he knows and likes people, and people like and trust him."

In an impromptu press session one day, LBJ was asked what it was really like to live in the White House and how his family life had changed. "You reach them by telephone," he said. "No one wants to say that the White House is not the most wonderful place to live. But you rarely see your wife, you rarely see your children. You rarely eat with them. You don't have a real family life. When you try to holler at one of them, it's kind of like hollering in a stadium—so you ask the White House operator, 'Get Lynda Bird.' "

Security details around the president had increased remarkably after the Kennedy assassination, but LBJ was known to grumble about them more often than not. He once said, "The thing I'm concerned about is, with thirty or forty Secret Service surrounding you, that one of their guns might go off. The people that give me the most trouble are the police and the Secret Service. They don't give me any protection. They just give me trouble." He said he came home one night and found five guards at his elevator. "I don't know what they would do in case of trouble," he said. "I guess they'd shoot each other."

In his book *LBJ: The Way He Was,* the late Frank Cormier, AP's White House correspondent, also reported Lyndon Johnson had a wariness of his Secret Service agents. Johnson used to tell reporters that if he ever got killed, it would not be because of an assassin, "it'll be some Secret Service agent who trips himself up and his gun goes off. They're worse than trigger-happy Texas sheriffs."

Maybe that's because he had heard a rumor that we reporters had heard when LBJ was vice president in the Kennedy administration. The alleged word from some of the agents was "If anything happens to Kennedy," turn around and shoot Johnson.

Still, LBJ knew people, he knew what the presidency meant to the people, and he truly enjoyed being able to let people in on some of the wonderful sides of the presidency. He loved to glide around the dance floor with an entranced partner in his arms, enjoying the music provided by the Marine Dance Band or other musical combos. In 1964, when he was seeking reelection, he tried to dance with all the wives of the members of the American Society of Newspaper Editors present at a White House reception. He wanted them to be able to go home and tell their friends, "I danced with the president of the United States."

At one private party early in his administration, he danced till 3 A.M., twirling one woman after another round the dance floor. Lady Bird's patience finally wore thin and she asked Tony Matarrese, the pianist and bandleader, to play "Goodnight Sweetheart." When Tony complied, LBJ stopped in the middle of the dance floor, glared at Tony, and stuck out his tongue. Tony just smiled and kept playing the first lady's request until everyone left.

Johnson always liked company, and one day I got to ride with him in the presidential helicopter. After sprinting several yards to get to the chopper on what was a breezy day, I settled myself into my seat. Johnson took one look at me, took a comb out of his pocket, and handed it over. "Here," he said. "Comb your hair. You're a mess."

The long strolls we took with LBJ around and around the South Lawn of the White House—which I used to call the Bataan Death Marches—were a new hazard in news conferences. As Al Spivak described the experience early on, "President Johnson has been bringing more newsmen to heel lately than his predecessors did in their combined history. His heel, their heel, each other's heel."

The distance was .29 miles for each circuit, and the unofficial champs were those who kept up with him through fifteen laps on August 26, 1964, the day of his nomination, the equivalent of four and a half miles. The lapsed time was an hour and a half—and LBJ managed to hold a full-blown news conference the entire time. As Al recalled, "Even the beagles Her and Him seemed a bit winded on the uphill legs of the walking tour." All of which prompted Al to compose a list of helpful hints for reporters who found themselves on "Bataan duty" on any given day:

"Dress lightly. Johnson generally chooses the days when the thermometer is above ninety for his strolls.

"Walk several steps ahead of the president. This is impolite but it is easier that way to hear Johnson's words. However, it does impose a slight strain on the neck, looking back all the time.

"Wear old shoes. Women should wear low heels. Men should bring shoeshine kits.

"Get a good night's sleep. Eat a hearty breakfast. And pay no attention to the fact that Johnson will go straight to the White House swimming pool while the news flock heads to its telephone booths."

On December 12, 1963, LBJ and Lady Bird held a social hour in the White House family quarters and invited a number of reporters and aides. LBJ played tour guide for all of us, showing us around, and in the Lincoln Bedroom, he remarked that the beds were made "big enough" back then, patted the mattress, and said, "It's got a good, firm mattress, too."

In Lynda's room, he showed off her collection of hundred-year-old dolls that had been given to her by LBJ's mother. In his room, the four-poster bed had a blue-and-white canopy; a small table nearby held a variety of newspapers. On a nearby chair were two dressing gowns for Lady Bird: one in green velvet trimmed in mink and the other in red. Next to them was a note, asking him which he liked best. "I haven't had time to decide," he said, "and told her she better keep them both."

It was a cold winter night, but that didn't stop him from taking us out onto the Truman Balcony for the incredible view.

He started reminiscing about his early days in Washington, how he had worked as an office clerk thirty-two years ago and come down with pneumonia. He remembered seeing Speaker Sam Rayburn dozing in a chair near him, cigarette ashes dropping onto his chest. Rayburn had come, LBJ said, because Rayburn and LBJ's father had been public servants together and Rayburn wanted to be there "in case anything happened to me."

Johnson spun a great yarn about Rayburn, whom the utility companies had labeled a radical because of legislation he was instrumental in passing. But for some unexplained reason, they invited him to speak at the Bond Street Club in New York, where, LBJ noted, "you had to be a millionaire to get in." They never expected Rayburn to accept but he did, and the person who introduced him said he wondered why Rayburn had accepted. Rayburn gave the crowd two reasons, LBJ said: (1) He was very poor as a young man and never could save any money, so he came to see all the millionaires because he thought it might rub off on him. And (2) "I came to show you I ain't scared of you."

We continued our tour through the Treaty Room, where LBJ recalled that Jackie Kennedy had cajoled him into giving her a chandelier for the room from the Capitol, and he had got it for her, he said, but "on loan." The room had a big, imposing desk and on it were a copy of Shakespeare's *Macbeth* and a geometry book. Lady Bird explained that Luci was using the room to do her homework but they were fixing up another location where she could study because "this room is too grand for that."

Someone asked LBJ how life had changed for him in Texas since he had become president, and he recalled that his cousin Oriole Bailey, who lived in a cottage on the ranch, was stopped by a Secret Service agent as she drove up to her home.

"How are you?" he asked.

"How am I? *Who* are you?" she countered. LBJ explained that she'd been there for seventy-five years but the Secret Service had been there "about seventy-five minutes."

It was quite a night and he ended our visit by noting, "I'm the thirty-sixth man to hold this job. Destiny put me here." He had not wanted it that way, he said, "but now that I'm here, I'm going to do the best I can."

"It's a very big place," sixteen-year-old Luci Johnson told me after the family had moved into the White House. "It's a very dark place. You can be just as happy as you want to be in it, or you can be miserable."

I had my own run-in with Cousin Oriole when I first called on her while LBJ was vice president. The great hostess Perle Mesta, two other reporters, and I were weekend guests at the Texas ranch and took a walk out to meet her. She came to the door in bare feet and a bathrobe, and afterward I wrote a story describing her home as "ramshackle" and mentioning her bare feet. She was furious and let LBJ know about it. "Does Helen Thomas sleep with her shoes on?" she asked the president.

I wrote a thank-you note after my visit and LBJ sent me the following:

"Dear Helen, I was down at Cousin Oriole's recently and you have no idea how much your story is in circulation along the Pedernales. Visitors just pass the ranch by now to stop at the most famous landmark of all, Oriole's house. You girls have an elevating influence, however. She sleeps with her shoes on, so no one will catch her otherwise. And after UPI referred to her house as 'ramshackle' she's hit me up for a paint job."

It was signed, "Affectionately, Lyndon B. Johnson."

During another visit to the ranch, Oriole picked up an astrological magazine, and as reported by AP's Frank Cormier, she kissed

Johnson on the top of his head and told him, "This magazine has your horoscope. It says you will be a good president but won't be reelected." Johnson laughed.

With all of today's talk of campaign finance reform and the incredible amounts of money raised and spent to get elected, LBJ had some notable contributions to his presidential campaign in 1964. The White House received letters from youngsters who not only voiced their support for the president but also backed it up with the coin of the realm. One letter arrived from a nine-year-old girl who wrote, "Dear Mr. President: A few weeks ago my cousin and I had a puppet show. We charged two cents for admission. Lots of people came. We earned sixty-two cents. Here it is for your campaign."

LBJ replied: "What a nice thing to do to earn money for the campaign. I appreciate so much your interest in me and I am sure the puppet show was a big success. Thank you and be sure to thank your cousin for me also."

The White House turned the contribution over to the Democratic National Committee and an aide reported, "It was handled just like any hundred-dollar or thousand-dollar donation."

One of LBJ's campaign techniques was to hardly ever directly mention by name or by title his opponent, Senator Barry Goldwater of Arizona. At a news conference in September, he grumbled to reporters, "If I say I love my mother, you would say it is a jab at Senator Goldwater."

After the 1964 election, Johnson threw a massive, Texas-style victory celebration at his ranch. Vice President–elect Hubert Humphrey flew in from Minnesota, and LBJ ordered up two horses. Humphrey gamely tried to ride along beside his boss, but he looked ill at ease and a groom finally led him and his horse back to the corral. As he dismounted, Humphrey stepped in some manure. "Mr. President," he exclaimed, "I just stepped on the Republican platform!"

As my UPI colleague Al Spivak wrote in a column shortly after LBJ won the election, "When Senator Hubert H. Humphrey takes the oath of office of vice president next January 20, he will be giving up his most cherished possession: the right of uninterrupted, unabashed, and unbeatable talk. From the Senate floor to the hustings, from the convention hall to the living room, the Minnesotan has built a reputation as one of America's champions of gab. His wit and—if a debate is hot enough—his tongue are considered among the sharpest in Washington. And the length of his speeches has left his audiences breathless, if not himself.

"But as vice president, Humphrey will be entering somewhat of a Silent Service, where he must live in the verbal as well as the professional shadow of his chief, President Johnson. When Humphrey visited Johnson at his ranch the day after the election, they both spoke at a victory barbecue. Their remarks were off-the-record but one humorist observed: 'This may be the first administration in history when a president will have to ask Congress to pass a law granting him equal time with the vice president.' "

Liz Carpenter, a former Texas newswoman and press secretary to Lady Bird Johnson, tells the story that when we were both out of college in the middle of World War II, we headed for Washington to become great journalists, we hoped. I had attended Wayne State University in Detroit and she had graduated from the University of Texas. We were confident we'd fulfill our dreams and find reporting jobs, but were short on money. Liz, who was always on the plump side, has a better story to tell on that score. She remembers wiring a message home to her brother:

"Please send me $200 or I'm going to have to sell my body." Her brother wired back: "Sell it by the pound." But he did send the money.

Two stories I always recall about the inimitable, wonderful Liz. At the height of the Vietnam War protests in 1968, she asked me how LBJ could win reelection. "Easy, Liz," I told her. "End the Vietnam War."

And when her White House days were over, we met for lunch. As Washington has always been the power center—for men—I was a little stunned when afterward Liz and I walked to the Northwest gate of the White House and I asked her, "What do you miss the most, Liz?"

"Power," she replied.

Once, on a Texas trip with LBJ, TV cameraman Tom Craven was driving about forty miles per hour and went through a speed trap. A police officer pulled him over and began to question him.

"Where you from?"

"I'm here following President Johnson," said Craven.

"Get along, buddy," said the officer. "You've got enough trouble."

When Lady Bird launched her historic "beautify America" project, little did we know she meant *all* of America. We logged more than one hundred thousand miles on those beautification trips with the first lady, who was later dubbed "secretary of the exterior."

On a raft trip on the Snake River in Wyoming, I was assigned to a raft called *Martini.* I quickly dubbed it *Martini on the Rocks* because that seemed to be where we spent most of our time. When her press entourage was photographed on that trip for a picture in *Sports Illustrated* magazine, you can spot me fairly easily—the most miserable-looking one of the bunch. We took the ride in a heavy downpour and had to take shelter under a tarpaulin for about three hours as we floated down the river.

Liz Carpenter remembers, however, my enterprising reporting skills on that trip: "Our boatman was Brent Eastman, a handsome outdoorsy type who had escorted Lynda occasionally. Naturally, the romantic-minded Helen stayed out in the rain to interview Brent while he paddled. The rest of us passed a handy bottle of whiskey 'for medicinal purposes' under the tarpaulin."

The humor columnist Art Buchwald was along on that trip and had shown up in Scottish golfer's outfit: woolen knickers, cap, plaid coat, and a pipe. He got drenched before the end of the ride. Liz asked him, "Art, what can I do to make you more comfortable?"

"Almost anything will make me more comfortable," he said.

One trip was to Big Bend National Park, probably one of the most remote parks in the U.S. park system. Getting there is not exactly half the fun: from San Antonio, it's four hundred miles to an abandoned airstrip left over from World War II. The 708,221-acre park is populated with jackrabbits, tarantulas, cougars, rattlesnakes, and antelope. In fact, before we landed, the pilot had to buzz the field twice to disperse a herd of antelope.

On the ground, there's another eighty miles by bus to the park's entrance and another fifteen miles to the motel, atop the appropriately named Ghost Mountains. Lady Bird said it was "the part of the world that was left over when the Lord made it."

Interior Secretary Stewart Udall was the guide for a three-mile hike along the Lost Mine Trail. Of course, we had to cover this trip, and to do that, we needed telephones. That involved stringing eighty miles of wire from Alpine, Texas. Still, Udall's assistant Charlie Boatner had a backup plan. He arranged to have a man with a donkey outside the pressroom wearing a sign: "Pony Express: Wire service copy here."

* * *

Sometimes those trips brought us into the realm of civilization. We visited the birthplace of John Quincy Adams in Massachusetts; Andrew Jackson's home, the Hermitage, in Tennessee; Thomas Wolfe's birthplace in Asheville, North Carolina; and Robert Frost's in Vermont. On one trip to Frost's home in Ripton, Mrs. Johnson paused at a marker and read aloud his poem "Mending Wall" engraved on a plaque:

> Something there is that doesn't love a wall,
> That sends the frozen ground swell under it.

A bit weary of the road show, I piped up and paraphrased another Frost line: "And we have miles to go before we sleep."

The first lady, recognizing the other lines by Frost, looked at the exhausted members of her loyal troupe and laughed.

In the 1964 presidential campaign, Johnson's challenger was the conservative senator from Arizona, Barry Goldwater. UPI reporter Bill Eaton covered Goldwater's campaign and reminded me that Lyn Nofziger, Goldwater's press secretary, handed out little gold-colored pins to the Washington-based reporters that read "Liberal Eastern Press." He also had matching pins that said "Western Conservative Press."

A bumper sticker spotted at the 1964 Republican National Convention: AuH_2O.

After his 1964 landslide victory over Goldwater, Johnson said of the election results, "I think it's very important that we have a two-party system. I am a fellow that likes small parties, and the Republican Party is about the size I like."

* * *

Let it not be said that George Bush and George W. Bush are the only presidents in modern history known to mangle their syntax. Reporters who covered LBJ's presidential campaign remember him repeatedly mispronouncing *tarpaulin* as he talked about the Russians wrapping their missiles and sending them home from Cuba in "tarpaulians."

Another nuclear-related mispronunciation prompted a couple of people who traveled with LBJ to make a fictional new game called Holy-Caust, which was supposed to involve the bombing of a mythical land called Tarpolia.

LBJ was without a doubt one of the most public presidents in modern history, but now and then his penchant for secrecy would give his staff and the press corps fits. Al Spivak recalled:

"One afternoon, [press secretary George Reedy] was asked whether Johnson's trip the next day to Groton, Connecticut, would encompass the keel-laying for a new atomic submarine. 'There are no plans to lay a keel,' Reedy told reporters. A reporter then told Reedy there had been reports that Johnson not only would lay the keel but that his LBJ initials would be branded on the sub. 'There are no plans to lay a keel,' Reedy replied. The next day, Johnson took part in a keel-laying ceremony, complete with the LBJ branding."

On May 28, 1964, confusion reigned when some reporters heard that LBJ was on his way to Arlington National Cemetery to visit President Kennedy's grave. Reedy said there was "nothing like that on the schedule" but he would look into the matter. "George, the Army says the president is at Arlington now," a reporter insisted at the briefing. "Is there any way you can check *now* to see if he is at Arlington *now*." So Reedy sent his assistant Malcolm Kilduff to check on the president in his office. Kilduff returned in a minute or two, whispered to Reedy, and

Reedy told the assembled press corps, "Mr. Kilduff informs me the president is not in his office."

"He's what?" another reporter asked from the back of the room.

"The president is not in his office," Reedy replied.

"Where is he?"

"Mr. Kilduff just brought back that piece of intelligence."

"George, doesn't somebody at the White House know where the president is?"

"Yes, somebody, of course, knows. I will have to find out for you."

Reedy telephoned LBJ's secretary while someone wondered out loud, "Who's in charge here?"

"He has left," Reedy announced after the phone call. "He has gone to the cemetery."

No president was more engrossed in the news than LBJ, so much so that he had three Teletypes in the Oval Office, which Nixon promptly removed when he came to power. But Johnson would be reading the stories as they came over the wire and was not hesitant to tell reporters when, in his opinion, they had got it all wrong.

While dictating a story one day, Frank Cormier of AP was interrupted by press secretary Pierre Salinger, who told him, "The president says to tell you you've got the wrong emphasis in your lead."

It was a love-hate relationship between the president and the press. Most of all he complained when his name was not on the front page every day.

I sometimes wonder what he would have done in the era of cell phones—have three in his pocket probably.

He also had a fondness for women reporters, thinking they would give him a better shake, telling them they were more "accurate." On one occasion, he told the newswomen they were "as good as the men reporters, maybe better," and gave us an exclusive on budget figures to prove it.

In the age of non-instant communication, most everyone knew about the "hot line" between Washington and Moscow. What it was exactly, however, had to be clarified once before a House Defense Appropriations subcommittee one year in LBJ's presidency. Under questioning by Representative Daniel Flood, Democrat of Pennsylvania, Major General G. P. Sampson explained that it was not a direct telephone hookup but a Teletype line, "and we send a test message to them [the Kremlin] every hour on the half hour and they send it to us every hour, roughly on the hour. The type message is something with no significance other than being composed of words in the English language. They send it back to us in the Russian language."

"The president is sitting at his desk," said Flood, "and for reasons best known to himself, instead of calling me in Wilkes-Barre, decides to call [Soviet leader] Khrushchev in Moscow. How does he do it? What happens? He has to pick up something?"

"He cannot pick up a telephone other than to make a commercial call," Sampson tried to explain. "The hot line is a Teletype, not voice. Messages have to be written. They are sent in English to Moscow over this."

"Where does the message originate?" asked Flood. "With the president?"

"Yes."

"What does he do? He writes it out. What does he do? Hand it to somebody?"

"He could hand it to somebody to take it down to the Washington terminal of the link," said Sampson.

"Where does it go from there?"

"Directly into the Kremlin."

"He writes something out and says, 'Good morning, Joe.' Then it goes to Moscow?"

"Yes, sir," said Sampson.

"Where does it arrive in Moscow?"

"I have been told in the Kremlin, sir," an increasingly and unfailingly polite Sampson replied.

But even LBJ got the "hot line" confused at times. At many, many stops in his forty-three-state, forty-thousand-mile campaign, he would frequently remind voters they had to decide "who do you want sitting next to that hot line when the telephone rings and somebody says, 'Moscow calling.' "

"For months and months," said an aide afterward, "we have tried to tell the public that the hot line isn't a telephone—it's a Teletype printer."

Other memories of that exhausting, grueling, and yet exhilarating campaign season were of LBJ always inviting folks to "come to the speakin'—bring your children, bring your dogs, and come on down to the speakin'." One night in Baltimore, though, he modified his message a bit to tell bystanders via a loudspeaker in his limousine, "Go on home and turn on your TV sets. I'm on television tonight."

At one stop in Milwaukee, LBJ burst into a grocery store and told a stunned proprietor, "I missed my lunch. Have you got a hunk of baloney sausage?"

Like her husband, Lady Bird was an indefatigable campaigner, and the "Lady Bird Whistlestop Campaign" was just as exhausting, grueling, and exhilarating as campaigning with her husband. We boarded the train, the Lady Bird Special, for a four-day trip that began in Alexandria, Virginia, went through North Carolina, South Carolina, Georgia, Florida, Alabama, and Mississippi, and ended up meeting Lyndon in New Orleans. We made sixty-seven stops and completed 1,682 miles over four days.

With many in the South opposed to the civil rights bill, Mrs. Johnson met the challenge in her first speech: "I know that many of you don't agree with the civil rights bill, or the president's support of it, but I do know the South respects candor and courage and I believe he has shown both. It would be a bottomless tragedy for our nation to be divided."

Along the route, we saw signs saying "Fly Away, Black Bird," and at a rally in South Carolina, hecklers tried to drown her out by shouting, "We want Barry." In a calm but strong voice, Lady Bird held up her hand and said, "In this country we have many viewpoints. You are entitled to yours. Right now, I'm entitled to mine."

LBJ had a similar campaign experience in Los Angeles, waiting for the hecklers to calm down and going so far as to urge his own people to stop trying to shout them down.

"Don't you Johnson people do that," he said. "Let's always be nice. When your neighbor comes over to your house, and he has been living there alone for a long time and he gets lonesome, and he comes to visit you, even if he does kind of start doing all the talking, you be nice to him and courteous. Because everybody is entitled to associate with good company once in a while.

"A fellow told me yesterday, I guess it was in Boston, they actually found an adult up there with one of those signs. We had about a thirty-three-mile caravan and they looked it all over very carefully, but they finally found one adult that had one of those signs.

"I asked him what was on it, and he said, 'Well, we thought it was an ugly sign until we got up close to where we could read.' It was a homemade sign and it said, 'Gold for the rich, and water for the poor, and Johnson for president.' "

As for all the hecklers LBJ encountered on the campaign trail, one reporter quipped at one point, "Johnson seems to get more Goldwater supporters at his rallies than Goldwater does."

*   *   *

George Reedy endured much with LBJ—all of his press secretaries did. But not much compared with the Christmas holiday when Mrs. Johnson's press secretary, Liz Carpenter, was absent and Reedy had to provide the assembled press with details about the first lady's gift and the Christmas decorations at the Texas White House. It should be noted that the acoustics in the press center weren't very good:

Reedy: The president's gift for the first lady, which he will be presenting tonight, is a simple gold brooch pin.

Q: Gold . . . what kind of . . . what? I didn't hear.

Reedy: A simple, gold brooch pin.

Q: Brooch?

(Reedy shrugged)

Q: Brooch . . . pin . . . that's redundant.

Reedy: Also rococo.

Q: Does it have any jewels or inscription on it?

Reedy: I am told it is a simple, gold brooch. (Laughter) The family Christmas-tree exchange of presents will be held on Thursday night, as it's the long-standing family custom to exchange gifts on Christmas Eve.

Q: Do they present them or do they open them?

Reedy: They usually open and exchange on Christmas Eve night.

Q: Do you know what is going in "Daddy's," "Mother's," "Lynda's," or "Luci's" socks?

Reedy: I don't know.

Q: They don't go into the socks on the tree?

Reedy: I do not know.

Q: Did you say the socks were on the tree?

Reedy: No, they are on the mantel.

Q: Where did you say the balsam boughs were, on the mantels?

Reedy: Mantels and the stairways. And also pinecones.

Q: Do you have anything else?

Reedy: That's all I have.

Newsman: Magnificent, George.

Another newsman: First-rate.

Reedy: Thank you.

Shortly after he underwent gallbladder surgery in 1965, LBJ invited a pool of reporters in to Bethesda Naval Medical Center to see him. A pressroom had been set up in a ward that housed mental patients, and when Johnson asked press secretary Bill Moyers what had happened to the patients, Moyers replied, "We gave them all press badges."

But Johnson's acute understanding of the importance of his health to the nation was underscored by Cousin Oriole when I asked her how she thought he looked.

"He looks tired," she said, "but he told me not to say that because I could start a depression."

Johnson also had surgery on his throat to remove a polyp, and as part of his recovery, doctors ordered him to stop talking for a few days. When the press asked Lady Bird how she felt about those orders, she smiled and said, "We're going to make the most of it."

A president often gets favorable responses from his generals, but he'll rarely get one from a reporter who asked the original question.

In 1967, LBJ recognized Al Spivak, who asked, "Will this [troop] increase, Mr. President, in whatever form it takes, fully meet the request that General Westmoreland has made?"

LBJ: The general can answer that as well as I can. But we have both answered it before. The answer is, yes, we have reached a meeting of the minds. The troops that General Westmoreland needs and requests, we feel if necessary, will be supplied. General Westmoreland feels that is acceptable, General Wheeler feels that is acceptable, and Secretary McNamara thinks that is acceptable. It is acceptable to me and we hope it is acceptable to you. Is that not true, General Westmoreland?

Westmoreland: I agree, Mr. President.

LBJ: General Wheeler?

Wheeler: That is correct, Mr. President.

LBJ: Secretary McNamara?

McNamara: Yes, sir.

LBJ: Mr. Spivak?

Al: Yes, sir.

At the 1966 Gridiron dinner, Humphrey's address touched on the vagaries of being a vice president. Describing his meeting with LBJ just after he had been selected as Johnson's running mate, Humphrey recalled, "The president looked at me and said, 'Hubert, do you think you can keep your mouth shut for the next four years?' I said, 'Yes, Mr. President,' and he said, 'Hubert, there you go, interrupting me again.'"

The actress Rosalind Russell once had dinner with Humphrey and remarked that the presidency was the most difficult job in the world. Humphrey insisted that his job was harder. "The president has only 190 million bosses," he told her. "The vice president has 190 million and *one.*"

When former British Prime Minister Winston Churchill died in 1965 at the age of ninety, Johnson was suffering from the flu, and his doctors ruled out a trip to London. It was assumed that Humphrey would head the U.S. delegation to the funeral, but instead Johnson slighted the vice president and sent Chief Justice Earl Warren.

We all felt that Johnson had a touch of jealousy and did not relish seeing Humphrey walking with kings and other potentates in the processional, especially if he couldn't be there.

At a news conference, Johnson was asked why Humphrey had not been designated to lead the U.S. delegation, especially when vice presidents are traditionally tapped for that role. Johnson was stunned and angry and remarked that he had not known the press was so interested in the protocol of state funerals. His weak response boiled down to his saying that when he was vice president, "I didn't go to everyone's funeral." But Churchill was in a different category, and Johnson—and we—knew it.

Longtime humorist Art Buchwald liked to say he had never been contacted directly by a president about one of his columns. However, he did say he had heard a story from White House aide Bill Moyers. One day Moyers was sitting at his desk, laughing out loud. LBJ happened by and stuck his head in Moyers's office, inquiring what was so funny. "I'm reading Buchwald," said Moyers. LBJ gave his aide one of those familiar glares. "You think he's funny?" he snapped.

"No, sir!" replied Moyers.

Buchwald struck again at the LBJ ranch, according to Frank Cormier, when White House press secretary Pierre Salinger was convulsed by an Art Buchwald column that zeroed in on some of the Johnson administration's foibles, and Salinger urged Johnson to read it. A few hours later Salinger encountered Johnson and asked him if he had read the column. Johnson said he had not.

Later, gathering Salinger and other members of his staff at lunch, Johnson asked Salinger to read the column aloud, "so we can all hear it."

Salinger's reading was greeted by a heavy silence. When he was finished, Johnson looked around the table and inquired, "Any of you all think that's funny?"

No one said a word.

* * *

Reporters today are getting their dose of religion from born-again President George W. Bush, but they never have to go to three church services on Sunday as we did while covering President Johnson in Texas. He would start out at his daughter Luci's Catholic church (she became a convert during her White House years) in Stonewall. Then on to Lady Bird Johnson's Episcopal church in Fredericksburg, a few miles away, followed by vesper services at the First Christian Church near the LBJ ranch, which was Johnson's church.

Kyle Thompson was UPI's Austin bureau manager when LBJ became president, and we relied on him whenever I, Merriman Smith, or Al Spivak traveled down to the Texas White House. Kyle recalled:

"LBJ loved to get down to his Texas ranch as often as possible, especially on holidays, when he could spend long days there. Helen and I usually stood what we called 'the church watch' on weekends, working out of a mobile home office behind the motel at Stonewall.

"Early in his presidency, Lyndon and Lady Bird would alternate Sundays at his church in Johnson City and her church in Fredericksburg. The latter, an Episcopal church, was very small with an old-fashioned front porch, not much unlike country homes. On one of those early Sundays, Helen and I were standing on this porch, looking through a window at the few people inside. LBJ and Lady Bird were sitting on the front bench, looking somewhat pious.

" 'Is the president a religious person?' Helen whispered to me.

" 'Not really, Helen, he just tolerates God,' I said. She giggled for about ten minutes.

"On another Sunday we were in our rented Plymouth following the LBJ station wagon to Fredericksburg, with the Secret Service black Mercury between us and the presidential car. Apparently LBJ ordered the Secret Service to slow us down, and he speeded up.

"I was driving, with Helen and [AP's] Fran Lewine in the front seat, and the Secret Service car slowed down, while the LBJ vehicle gradually pulled out of sight.

"I tried two or three times to pass the Secret Service car, and it would pull over, preventing same. So I told Helen and Fran to 'hold on' and suddenly swerved to the left and managed to pull up beside them. We both floored the accelerators and got up to about ninety miles per hour before the Secret Service gave up and let us pass. We caught LBJ before they arrived at church, and I stuck my hand out and motioned the Secret Service car to get into its proper spot between us and LBJ. When we arrived at the church, the Secret Service guys bailed out, grinning somewhat sheepishly. Helen and Fran got a big kick out of that incident. These things helped keep our church watch duty from being too boring."

That LBJ was an extremely demanding boss is gross understatement. A compulsive workaholic, he couldn't stand to see anyone standing idly by. Liz Carpenter recalled that early in his presidency, the Secret Service increased the size of the detail guarding him at his ranch in Texas. All told, there were about thirty agents, "and one day the president walked into the kitchen and found them all standing around drinking coffee—*his* coffee. And that made him crazy. He wanted them to be doing something.

"So he turned around, just bristling, and he yelled at them, 'Swat flies!' They all stared at him for a moment. Then Rufus Youngblood, the chief of the White House detail, picked up a flyswatter and said, 'Well, I guess flies *are* a security problem.'"

LBJ had Air Force One reconfigured so he had a desk similar to the one he had in the Oval Office, with a push-button bar. He would pour his own drink, a Scotch—he claimed he drank bourbon and branch water because it fit the Western image, but he preferred Scotch. Then he would lean back, lift his feet on the desk, and say to press secretary George Reedy, "Gawge, bring the boys in here."

Without fail when I heard him, I would correct him, directly and respectfully: "We're not all boys, Mr. President."

Traveling on Air Force One would spoil anyone, but what many may not realize is that for some time it was the president's plane, period. Many times in earlier administrations we flew on chartered aircraft, and one trip to Ohio is still with me today. Lady Bird, accompanied by Liz, other staff members, and a ten-person news entourage, was traveling to a senior citizens' residence, and we ended up with tourist-class tickets aboard a United Airlines jet. On the way to Cleveland, there were black storm clouds on all sides. As we bounced around, Liz rang for the flight attendant and asked her, "When are we going to get out of this?"

"Out of what?" she said.

Lady Bird, who had sunk her head into a pillow, looked up and said, "She means when will this plane stop jiggling?"

"I'll check," said the attendant, and headed to the cockpit. At that point there were two flashes of lightning, the plane began shaking crazily, and there was a loud—very loud—clap of thunder. We must have bounced around like that for nearly half an hour. Finally—finally—we landed. Fran Lewine and I, pale and shaken as we were, got hold of the pilot. Yes, the plane had been struck by lightning but there was no damage, we were told. We went outside, looked at the blackened motor, and headed to the airport to phone in our bulletins: "First Lady's Plane Struck by Lightning."

For the trip home, Lady Bird put the decision to a vote, and we opted for an eleven-hour drive back to Washington. Liz did not let the Secret Service personnel have a vote "because," she recalled, "I didn't want the cowards to be outvoted by the courageous."

They rented six cars—nicely outfitted with pillows, blankets, and whiskey, "for medicinal purposes," of course.

We stopped at a Howard Johnson's outside Pittsburgh for a bite to eat, as the White House team had called ahead and asked to "reserve a table for Mrs. Johnson and party."

As we were leaving, one of the reporters asked a waitress, "How did you feel serving Mrs. Johnson?"

"Well, I was pretty nervous," she said.

"Have you ever met a first lady before?"

"First lady?" the stunned waitress said. "First lady?"

"Yes, that was Mrs. Lyndon B. Johnson."

"Oh, my God," the waitress said. "Thank goodness I didn't know it. I would have fainted dead away. I thought it was Mrs. Howard Johnson—that was bad enough!"

Al Spivak traveled with LBJ on a trip to California to boost the candidacy of Pierre Salinger. After he'd left the White House, where he had served as press secretary for both Kennedy and Johnson, Salinger declared his candidacy for a U.S. Senate seat in California. Johnson, who never had any trouble embracing congressional candidates, went the extra mile for Salinger's campaign. At a Democratic fund-raiser in San Francisco, Johnson told the crowd, "You are going to have another effective senator, and he will be able to run into the White House almost as fast as he ran out." Salinger, who had resigned in March to run in the primary, had given LBJ just a few hours' notice of his impending departure.

While it was an amiable parting, LBJ was unhappy to see him leave at the time. Johnson had wanted to keep as many of Kennedy's political team around as he could.

Salinger went on to defeat state comptroller Alan Cranston for the nomination and ran against Republican George Murphy.

"I want to confess," LBJ told the crowd, "that I was somewhat surprised when Pierre told me he intended to run for senator in a state that is more than five hundred miles long. It was just a few months ago that he refused to walk even fifty miles."

A few days later, LBJ invited Salinger to fly back to Washington with him, and the two spent a few hours together in the private presidential cabin. Of course, Salinger had flown aboard Air Force One many times with Kennedy and LBJ, but never as a candidate. With the new situation, he seemed genuinely thrilled about having the Johnson glamour rub off on him.

As Al wrote, "The best example of this was when Salinger, who has set up many a photograph for Democratic candidates beside the president, finished a day of standing with, sitting with, walking with, and motorcading with Johnson. Salinger approached several cameramen at one point and excitedly asked, 'Did you get us both in the picture?'"

Al also wrote a wonderful piece in 1965 about LBJ's habit of perpetually using the telephone. He would call anyone, anywhere, anytime. However, when he did pick up that phone, he expected to hear a female voice on the other end—he liked hearing female voices, and it was what he was used to at the White House—asking him, "Number, please." When he was at the Texas ranch, he had to deal with male telephone operators on the vacation White House switchboard. That operation was run by the Army Signal Corps, which handled other White House communications operations. So, on his latest visit to Texas, three of the female civilian operators from the regular White House switchboard were sent to Johnson City to handle the telephone circuits.

"This, it would seem, will be the standard arrangement when the president is out of town for any time," Spivak wrote. "A special White House switchboard is always set up at the ranch or at Camp David or anyplace the chief executive stays. Even if the visit is only for a few minutes, White House telephones are installed and hooked into leased commercial lines for instant contact with Washington. The president thus can be contacted in case of a crisis or can place calls affecting the nation's business without delay.

"All of this is standard procedure and related only indirectly to Mr. Johnson's reputation as a perpetual telephoner. This gave rise, when he was Senate Democratic leader, to an anecdote about his limousine and the telephone in it. When Senator Everett M. Dirksen [Republican of Illinois], so the story goes, became Senate Republican leader and got a limousine with a mobile telephone, he decided to call Mr. Johnson.

" 'Hullo, Lyndon,' Dirksen is reported to have said. 'I am in my limousine and I thought I'd give you a call on my telephone while I'm riding.'

" 'Hullo, Ev,' Mr. Johnson is supposed to have replied. 'I'm in my limousine, too. But would you hold on a minute please? My other phone is ringing.' "

With his polls plummeting in 1968, Johnson decided to mock them and the idea that one could govern by paying attention to them. At the Gridiron dinner—which was held in Old Williamsburg that year—Johnson said, "The statesmen of Williamsburg were some of our first political analysts, and it was here that a special courier first delivered the advance release which referred to Patrick Henry's private poll from his home district: 'Forty-six percent for liberty, fifteen percent for death, fifteen percent undecided.'

"I've been reading a lot about my own polls in the newspapers, and I'm worried it could be I've peaked too soon."

To commemorate Lady Bird's longtime project, beautifying America, she and her husband traveled to northern California in 1970 and stood with President and Mrs. Nixon in a magnificent redwood forest. The ceremony was to commemorate Nixon's signing of a proclamation declaring the three-hundred-acre tract the "Lady Bird Johnson Grove," in honor of her tireless efforts to preserve America's natural landscape.

As the four stood together, Nixon observed the similarities between himself and LBJ in their respective political histories: congressman, senator, vice president, president.

"Presidents are lonely people," LBJ said to Nixon. "The only ones they are sure of all the time are their women kinfolk."

"Yes, and we're both fortunate in the fact that we married above ourselves," Nixon replied.

Leonard Marks also told what could be termed a typical "Johnson treatment" story, and how he was appointed head of the U.S. Information Agency. One day in July 1965, he got a call from Johnson about 10 A.M.: "With no introduction he said that he was announcing my appointment as director of USIA at a press conference at noon.

"I told him he couldn't do that to me. I was at the height of my career. I was enjoying myself, and my wife would never understand. He said he would hold off a day so I could explain it to her. Do you know when he made the announcement? At noon.

"That was so typical of Johnson. He would not take no for an answer. And he usually caught his potential appointees by surprise. He hated to be scooped by the press and would even cancel the appointment if it leaked in the newspapers before he could announce it."

As much as he liked being in the White House, LBJ was known to reflect on the more sober side of living there. In a speech in Texarkana, the Texas-Arkansas border city, he reflected, "Sometimes in the late of night, when all the capital city has gone to sleep, I sit by myself behind that big black fence and I read and I think, and oftentimes it is so quiet in the White House that I can almost hear the footsteps of the men who have lived in that house, and the men who have walked its halls and have slept in its rooms and have stayed awake waiting for the sun to come up . . . Jefferson, Madison, Jackson, Abraham Lincoln, Theodore Roosevelt, Woodrow Wilson, Franklin D. Roosevelt, Harry Truman, Dwight Eisenhower, and John Fitzgerald Kennedy."

A few days later at another speech in Eufaula, Oklahoma, he told the crowd:

"Not many of you get waked up in the night about Cyprus, or Zanzibar or Vietnam. But I never send a reconnaissance mission out about eleven o'clock, with our planes and our boys guiding them to take a look at what is developing, and realize they have to be back at three-thirty in the morning, but what promptly at three twenty-five I wake up without an alarm clock. Because I want to be sure my boys got back, and sometimes they don't come back."

In an interview with the American Bar Association's magazine, Leonard Marks recalled the day he went to see Johnson and told him, " 'Mr. President, we're getting the hell kicked out of us all around the world. There's adverse comment about our participation in Vietnam. The headlines, radio broadcasts, they're all condemning us. I say we get out and bring the boys home. That's what I'd do.' In all the time I knew him, he never said a cross word to me, but that day he told me to get out of the room.

"Although I was not a statutory member of the National Security Board, LBJ ordered that I was to sit at the table. I attended all sessions and voiced the USIA positions. After that experience, I no longer received notices about the meetings.

"I was ready to resign when Lady Bird called and invited my wife and me to a surprise party for LBJ.

"I went with trepidation, but as soon as he saw me, Johnson put his arm around me as though nothing had happened. He told a fellow partygoer, 'This is the brightest man in my government—the most loyal friend I have.' And all of a sudden, I got notices about the meeting again.

"After he left office and retired to his ranch, I continued to be his lawyer. One weekend when I was at the LBJ ranch, I asked him why he got mad at me. He said, 'Because I knew you were right and there was nothing I could do about it. I couldn't get out of Vietnam, I inherited it. Kennedy's people were still in government. There would have been a huge uproar in the House and Senate, I couldn't get out.'"

I have learned a lot about presidents, and one thing is sure. None will ever admit there is a change in policy. The world can change but they always insist that they are on the same course, steering steadily. None have learned that consistency is the hobgoblin of small minds.

It's also tough to admit a mistake. Johnson in particular would never admit a change even if it was a 180-degree turn. It's point of pride and perhaps a president's own belief in his infallibility. Perhaps it is a feeling that changing one's mind means weakness.

Johnson used to tell us over and over again that he wanted to be the "president of all the people."

He also used to remind us, "I'm the only president you've got." When he would say this at the height of the Vietnam War, I would say under my breath, "Help."

On space, Johnson wrote that while he was in charge of the space program, he stayed in close touch with the astronauts: "They represent the best this nation can produce; they are the folk heroes of our time."

He also proposed that nations make the exploration of outer space "a joint venture." During his presidency, he signed two space treaties with the Soviet Union and many other countries. One treaty provided for the safe return of any nation's astronauts and space equipment landing within the jurisdiction of another nation. The other banned weapons of mass destruction from outer space. "These two treaties can help remove causes of future friction from the realm of outer space," he said.

When it came to social policy, Johnson's achievements stand out as among the greatest of the last half of the twentieth century. He put all his chips in to pass the Medicare program and got it passed despite a flood of forecasts of disaster.

Before signing the bill, he called John Gardner, Secretary of Health, Education, and Welfare, and told him, "John, if you're wrong in your calculations, we're both going to look like the worst damned fools."

"I hope you're not worried," Gardner replied.

"No," Johnson replied. "If a man can't take that kind of chance, he doesn't belong in public life."

Johnson knew that the landmark laws he proposed and promoted for his Great Society would be his lasting legacy. In his book *The Vantage Point: Perspectives of the Presidency, 1963–1969*, he wrote:

"I was haunted to the last days of my presidency by the work still undone in both health and education, and I continue to be concerned. I am deeply troubled that we, the richest nation on earth, are still fifteenth in infant mortality. I am distressed that 750,000 poverty-stricken women do not receive adequate medical care during pregnancy. Think of the burdens life imposes on their babies just to survive."

When LBJ's presidency was drawing to a close, a friend asked George Reedy, his first press secretary, what Johnson would do after he left the White House. Given the president's love of power, said the friend, where would LBJ go and what would he do?

Reedy puffed on his pipe for a minute, then said, "Have you thought of pope?"

* * *

So many times, Johnson used to tell us, "I'm going home, where they take care of you when you're sick and they care when you die."

That's how Johnson approached his own final years. He went home to his beloved Texas. When LBJ left the White House, AP reporter Saul Pett and I traveled with the family on the flight home. Saul and I had asked for an interview on board and we sat with LBJ. Saul asked him, "At what moment did you feel that you were no longer president, after Nixon was sworn in?"

Johnson looked at his hands for a moment, then said, "Four seconds afterward, I felt differently."

On that flight, Luci handed me a note:

"Helen:

"I'm truly glad to see you here—you really have gone all the way with the LBJs—and it means a lot."

RICHARD M. NIXON

President Nixon had a sense of humor of sorts, but his remarks and answers at presidential news conferences usually had a touch of bitterness. Most of the time he displayed downright hostility to the press.

It was a throwback to his first entry into national politics and it got worse as the years went on. The strains with the press did not make for many laughs, but at times he did try to lighten up and reach out—though often it was too late.

Nixon was not one for small talk. His forte was speaking before political gatherings, where he could show his stuff.

He was also comfortable with a small coterie of friends, but even his closest comrades could not remember many laugh lines. To Richard Nixon, life was real, life was earnest.

When Nixon was vice president, he made a trip to London and someone forgot to pack his dinner suit. Nixon ended up renting one but had to settle for a suit that was three sizes too large, as every rentable tux had already been spoken for. A colleague recalled the headline that appeared in the *Victoria* (Texas) *Advocate* about Nixon's sartorial effort: "Queen Elizabeth Radiant as Dick Twitches in Baggy Pants."

Nixon aide and loyalist Lyn Nofziger once even admitted, "I sometimes lie awake at night trying to think of something funny that Richard Nixon said."

* * *

According to Lou Cannon, the longtime White House correspondent for the *Washington Post,* a former colleague of Nixon's in the House of Representatives and other lawmakers decided to throw him a party when he was serving as vice president. They called his secretary, Rosemary Woods, and told her that they'd like some "funny stories" about Nixon so they could regale the crowds at the forthcoming party. Woods paused for a moment and then said, "There *are* no funny stories about Mr. Nixon."

Maybe the comedian Mort Sahl was onto something with a joke he told many years ago: "When the nation was founded, we had about two million people and yet we produced Washington, Adams, Jefferson, Madison, Franklin, Lee, John Marshall, so many others. Now we've got two hundred million people and the best we can do is Nixon and Agnew. What can we learn from this? Darwin was wrong."

When Nixon took office, I noted that the women of the press corps found Pat more relaxed and at ease than when her husband had been vice president. In an interview, I wrote, "She is warm and kind and she goes the extra mile to shake a hand and greet a stranger. She is concerned about people's feelings. As a hostess, she has kept her promise of not entertaining just the big shots. She never forgets her days of poverty when she was growing up."

When a new administration prepares to take over the White House, a certain housekeeping job always has to be addressed. It's politely referred to as the resignation procedure. All cabinet members and top political appointees are expected to resign by Inauguration Day and allow the incoming chief executive to put together his own management team.

When Ronald Reagan was preparing to leave office, his chief of staff, Kenneth Duberstein, delivered the message to administration officials at a breakfast meeting—and Reagan himself reminded his staff at an afternoon session. An aide said that during the morning meeting, Secretary of State George Shultz, also a veteran of the Nixon administration, expressed his gratitude for the "dignity" and civility with the way things were handled.

Shultz also recalled that Nixon, the day after he was reelected in 1972, assembled his cabinet and aides and told them, "Now I have to go to Camp David." His chief of staff, H. R. Haldeman, then passed out a resignation form letter that each member was ordered to sign. And then Haldeman told the assembled group, "You're all a bunch of burned-out volcanoes."

Early in his first term, we had heard—as we'd heard before—that this was going to be an "open administration." In his first year in office, Nixon told reporters he would hold a news conference only when it was "in the public interest." He rarely thought they were, averaging about seven a year during his first term, sometimes going four or five months without one.

When he did hold a press conference, he prepared for it diligently, studying briefing papers several days in advance and having his staff hold mock sessions. Still, we were accused by White House aide John Ehrlichman of asking "soft, flabby questions." Later we understood the criticism came from Nixon, who complained that we never asked "hard" questions.

So I was flattered when, in an interview in that first administration, Nixon told me, "You always ask tough questions, tough questions not in the sense of being unfair but hard to generalize the answers."

Nixon always seemed happier when he was on a plane heading out of the country. He loved the pomp and ceremony that went along with such tours. One summer, however, we were all sweltering in New Delhi and Nixon spoke of the warmth of welcome he had received.

"Well, sir," said Prime Minister Indira Gandhi, "you came at the wrong time of day and the wrong time of year."

On a trip to Yugoslavia, President Tito took Nixon on a tour of his birthplace, leading him through his ancestral home and then pointing to a mahogany cradle.

"My bed," he told Nixon.

"Do you remember where you were born?" Nixon asked.

Tito then motioned for Nixon to sit with him on a bench around an old concrete furnace that his family had used to keep warm in the cold winter. He pointed to a rifle overhead and told Nixon that he had used it to protect his family's vineyards.

"Against animals?" asked Nixon.

"No," said Tito, "against people."

Then it was on to a wall of family pictures and Tito pointed to a photograph of himself as a "partisan" fighter in World War II and showed Nixon a "most wanted" poster with his picture and the price the Nazis had put on his head.

"One hundred thousand marks!" exclaimed Nixon.

"Gold marks," corrected Tito.

"Were you worth it?" Nixon asked.

Tito just looked at him, smiled slightly, and walked away.

"My parents were Quakers. They didn't believe in this sort of thing," said President Nixon after dancing publicly for the first time with his wife, Pat, at daughter Tricia's wedding in 1971.

An example of Nixon's bitter humor took place during his breakthrough trip to China in 1972. We reporters were able to cover Nixon and the suave Chinese leader Chou En-lai at a photo op before they marched into the Great Hall for a mammoth banquet. As they clinked their glasses, Chou asked reporters if they were having a good time.

Nixon could be heard in an offstage whisper, "More than they deserve."

And when we were in a government guesthouse to witness the start of a meeting, Chou encouraged photographers to take more pictures.

"If they do take them, they will only burn them," said Nixon.

During the trip to China, I covered Pat Nixon visiting one of the communes and the first lady recalled her own early life on a farm. As we looked into a pigpen, she wondered aloud what kind of pigs they were.

"Male chauvinist, of course," I piped up. Everyone in the party, except for the Chinese, cracked up. The Chinese were not familiar with the feminist jargon of that era.

At a weekend at Camp David, Nixon came in one afternoon and announced to Secretary of State Henry Kissinger, "I scored 121."

"Your golf is improving, Mr. President," said Kissinger.

"I was bowling!" Nixon snapped.

Even after the House Judiciary Committee voted articles of impeachment, Pat remained unswervingly loyal. "You know I have great faith in my husband," she told me, clenching her fists. "I happen to love him." She wanted him to fight on, but when he decided on resignation, she set to work at once planning the move out of the White House. She thought he should have burned the incriminating tapes during the Watergate crisis and wanted to fight to the end against removal from office. When she died of lung cancer in June 1993, she had already composed her epitaph: "I just want to be remembered as the wife of a president."

Well, I guess we should have seen it coming from Vice President Spiro Agnew. "I apologize to you. . . . And I promise I won't deceive you except in matters of this sort." He was speaking to reporters about his assertion that he would not be traveling to Cambodia—on a plane that was headed to Phnom Penh.

A former colleague of mine recalled that in the 1970s, Vice President Agnew wrote an op-ed piece "about the economy or Vietnam—or something. The following Sunday, there was a correction in the Week in Review section saying, 'An op-ed piece last week should have carried the note, "Mr. Agnew is vice president of the United States." ' "

After Vice President Agnew resigned, one of the big questions was who would be his successor. We tried every trick in the book to pry the name, any name, out of anyone who might be privy to the information. James Naughton of the *New York Times* approached Joe Laitin and asked him to help confirm a tip he'd received about Agnew's successor. He told Joe he had the information "cold," but his informant, in an understandable mood of self-preservation, would only give James the VIP license plate number.

However, the government classifies VIP licensees as top secret, and only the Secret Service and the FBI can release such information. Joe enlisted the aid of an FBI agent assigned to the White House (George Saunders) and assured him there would be no problem involving national security, got the name, and passed it along to James.

Meanwhile, things were reaching fever pitch at the White House, which was supposed to announce Agnew's successor shortly. As Joe told the story, "Naughton had gotten his tip from an 'unimpeachable' source and I was impressed with the way his source was protecting himself. I gave him the name of the VIP licensee in as casual a tone as I could—Judge John J. Sirica."

A UPI colleague David Rosso reminded me of a note he sent in 1992: "Twenty-one years ago I was still new to D.C. and UPI and, while working the switchboard, Stan Hall told me to get the Watergate. I said, 'What's the Watergate?' 'Everybody knows what the Watergate is,' Hall said. This was a year before I was on the Metro desk and wrote the first story about a break-in at the DNC headquarters at the Watergate, and then everybody really did know what Watergate was."

Anything can happen in the White House, and during the unraveling of Watergate, nearly anything did. One day Joe Laitin was walking into the basement en route to a routine meeting with George Shultz, whose office was in the West Wing. Joe rounded a corner and said he was "almost knocked over by a man with a wild look of desperation, grim-faced, bent over, fists clenched. He brushed hard against me, and before I could regain my balance, I was instantly surrounded by a dozen equally desperate men who whooshed past me in hot pursuit.

"At first I thought I'd blundered into some Keystone Kops chase being reenacted for a movie. It took me a few seconds to realize I'd almost been bowled over by the president of the United States and again by his Secret Service detail. Something was up. It was obvious President Nixon had bolted from the Oval Office and caught the Secret Service off guard—not an easy thing to do. Now he was charging in a state of fury and frenzy to his hideaway quarters in the Old Executive Office Building.

"I dusted myself off, then slowly exited the White House basement, heading back to my office in the same building the president was now ensconced. The country was in the throes of the Watergate scandal, and here I was a fly on the wall observing history. I had been summoned by my boss on a routine matter. By now, twenty minutes later, I couldn't even remember what it was for, nor had his secretary inquired why I hadn't shown up. Sitting at my desk, I was still numbed by the encounter. The specter of the hollow stare in Nixon's eyes, as he lurched past, had frozen me into a catatonic state. Finally my body relaxed.

"Without thinking, I reached for the phone and dialed. It was a private number to the Secretary of Defense. I asked if the president could order the use of atomic weapons without consulting him or the Joint Chiefs. The answer was yes. I inquired whether the president, as commander in chief, could, without notifying the Joint Chiefs, order combat troops to surround the White House. Again the answer was affirmative. I asked him to please listen to me for five minutes without interruption and without comment. He must have thought I'd gone gaga.

"All he said was 'Make it fast.' I explained I'd just had an encounter with the president that left me unsettled and truly concerned about the president's stability. If I were Secretary of Defense, I said, I'd want an understanding with the Joint Chiefs that no one would issue an 'execute' order involving atomic weapons without mutual consultation. Then I would determine whether the commander of combat-ready troops geographically closest to Washington would take orders from the president without question. And then, as a precaution, I would want to know the location of the next-nearest combat-ready troops capable of overpowering the first contingent and whose commanding officers would be loyal to the chain of command.

"Looking back, you'd think I was talking about some impending revolution in a banana republic, not the USA. I ended with 'That's all I have to say.'"

Much later, it came to light that an alert did go out and commanders were ordered not to take any direct orders from the White House.

When it comes to a cover-up, cover it up with a remark like President Nixon's in 1973: "That is, because of, because of our, that is, we are attempting, the position is to withhold information and to cover up—this is totally true—you could say this is totally untrue."

* * *

UPI correspondent Bill Cotterell shared this sports story from the Watergate days: "The University of Florida and Florida State University used to give us free grandstand tickets. In 1973, I drove over to Jacksonville to help Stan Darden cover the Georgia-Florida game, and we each had a pair of tickets and no guests.

"We decided it wouldn't be ethical to take money for them, so after we got our lunch and set up in the press box, I took the four tickets down to the parking lot where the scalpers were, holding them aloft and waving the tickets.

"A guy in a fraternity windbreaker came up and said, 'How much?' and I said he could have them free. He looked over at his buddy and their dates across the street, turned the tickets over, eyed me suspiciously, asked a couple more times, 'No, really?'

"I explained that Stan and I had our press box passes and didn't feel it'd be right to sell the tickets we got free from the universities. Finally, he called his friends over and they solemnly shook my hand like I'd cured some terrible affliction for them.

"As they walked away, the first guy came back and shook my hand again and said, 'We're not going to listen to what Nixon and Agnew say about the press anymore.'"

Gene Hintz, who served time in Wisconsin for UPI, recalled this story:

"I spent time alone with him a couple of times when he felt the press didn't 'have Dick Nixon to kick around anymore.'

"The first was in the midsixties when I believe he was practicing law in California. Anyway, he was brought in to address a Wisconsin State Bar convention. I was the only media member to show up, and the bar—not having any love for the media anyway—stuffed me into a small anteroom off the convention hall. I looked around and there was Dick, waiting to make his speech.

"After introductions, he asked what I covered for UPI, and since it was fall, one of the things I mentioned was Green Bay Packers football. That was all that was needed. He started asking questions about one of his heroes [Vince Lombardi] and wouldn't let up. I hardly could get enough questions in to get a story.

"Sadly, I didn't have the guts to tell him what Lombardi [a JFK backer] really thought of him. It hadn't been too long before that when at a postpractice social with the coaches, the news came on. For some reason or another, Nixon appeared on the screen. From across the room came a roar: 'Turn that g—d—— thing off. I never want to see that man again!' The set went off. When Vince Lombardi ordered something, it was done.

"About two or three years later, Nixon surprised me. The only time I'd seen him was in that half-hour meeting, and he was returning to Milwaukee for another speech. While he hadn't announced for president yet, there was speculation. When he stepped into the room, there was no question about it. He was wearing Pan-Cake makeup! He strode up to me, shocked me by remembering my name, and then chatted briefly with a few other reporters.

"My first question was whether he was looking forward to [like LBJ] a White House wedding [a reporter's oblique way of asking him whether he planned to run for president]. He hedged his answer, and it was a few months later he announced. Still one strange man. I never did see him after that."

After Nixon resigned, he was hospitalized with phlebitis and developed a clot in his leg. Bill Cotterell was in Washington and near the White House spotted what he described as "a filthy VW microbus covered with hand-painted flowers, et cetera, what we used to call a hippie van. There were faded bumper stickers that said 'Free Angela Davis,' 'Free the Chicago 7,' and 'Free Huey Newton.'

"The only clean spot on the van was a new sticker that said 'Free the Clot.' "

* * *

UPI's Sue Morgan recalls a bumper sticker she saw in a parking lot in Chicago during the Watergate era: "Don't Blame Me: I'm from Massachusetts." It was the only state George McGovern carried in the 1972 election.

Adversarial can be a mild term to describe how presidents feel about their relationship with reporters. With Richard Nixon, it took on a whole new dimension. As events related to Watergate unfolded every day, the disclosure of Nixon's "enemies list" of Washington correspondents was in a class by itself.

When the list became public, it was noted that one man on it was dead. I almost landed on the list myself when I asked press secretary Ron Ziegler, "How did he die?"

One of the braver moments in Watergate history: In discussing how they could avoid subpoenas, Nixon's chief of staff, H. R. Haldeman, remarked, "We move to Camp David and hide. They can't get in there."

In February 1974, President and Mrs. Nixon attended the nineti-eth birthday party for Alice Roosevelt Longworth, and Nixon presented her with a paper bag. "It's two jars of Iranian caviar. The Shah sent it to Pat and it's from her to you. Eat it with a spoon."

"I'll wallow in it," said Mrs. Longworth.

When it was time to leave, Nixon told the guest of honor, "I hope I'll see you before the year is up. Do you still refuse calls until afternoon? That's good. Don't talk on the phone until afternoon."

"I like him," Mrs. Longworth said later. "He'll never resign or be impeached."

During the Senate Watergate hearings, Senator Sam Ervin asked a young White House aide what he would tell any other young man who was thinking about going into public service.

"I'd tell him to stay away," said the aide.

* * *

It was Valentine's Day, 1974, and no one had seen the president for weeks. That night I got a tip that Nixon and his wife, Pat, were at Trader Vic's restaurant, a few blocks away from the White House. Lesley Stahl of CBS and I got together and grabbed a table near the Nixons and their friend Bebe Rebozo. As they got up to leave, Lesley and I ran out ahead of them, hoping to ask a few questions. However, news had traveled fast, and by the time we got on the outdoor escalator, television and still cameras were crowding the area.

As the first couple emerged, Lesley and I got pushed farther to the back as the cameras closed in. We looked to our left and saw Pat standing all alone, also crowded out by the crush of cameras.

We approached her and I said, "How are you?" Her eyes welled up with tears. "Helen," she said, "can you believe that with all the troubles Dick has had, all the pressures he's been under, he would do this for *me?*"

In May 1984, when Walter Mondale was seeking to challenge Ronald Reagan for the presidency, Nixon was asked to speak at a luncheon for the American Society of Newspaper Editors. Of course, Watergate came up and someone asked him what was the most significant lesson he had learned from that experience.

"I lived it at the time and lived it in my memories and recent broadcasts," he said. "As far as I'm concerned, I've covered the subject as well as I can. I think ten years of Watergate is enough. I'm concerned with the future, not the past."

He also predicted that Walter Mondale would win the Democratic nomination on the first ballot and that the race against President Reagan "will be closer than they think," but he also thought Reagan would win "because he's a better candidate."

The choice of Geraldine Ferraro to be the vice presidential candidate, he said, would not help Mondale because "activist type of women" were already backing him. Nixon predicted Mondale "will bow toward women and not take one on the ticket because it wouldn't help him." He said Mondale could name either Senator Gary Hart of Colorado or Senator Lloyd Bentsen of Texas as his running mate, but speculated that Hart would be more helpful to the ticket.

And Nixon predicted Mondale would win the presidential debates but Reagan "would win the audience."

When asked about that famous "enemies list," Nixon said he did not make one up (he didn't say who did, but a few have attributed it to H. R. Haldeman), but that didn't mean that all the media names on the list were his friends. "I was president at a controversial period. They didn't like what we were trying to do. I have no enemies in the press corps."

He also said he didn't know whether there was a "new Nixon" or a "reincarnation, but there is an old one and I feel old."

Jesse Jackson, who also was a presidential contender that year, addressed the group before Nixon did. He complimented the newspaper editors, saying they had shown a "redemptive spirit" by inviting Nixon. "Somebody might suggest you all should repudiate him," said Jackson. "He brought shame and disgrace at one point to our country, but he has been redeemed and all human beings are worthy of redemption."

Bob Schieffer, the host of CBS's *Face the Nation,* once noted how presidents came and went and no matter who was in office, I stayed "politely respectful but unintimidated." Bob recalled that at a news conference with Secretary of State Henry Kissinger one day, the secretary announced that he couldn't really explain what he had to say in the twenty minutes that were allotted to him.

"Why don't you just start at the end," I suggested.

* * *

At a news conference close to the end of Nixon's presidency in 1974, press secretary Ron Ziegler noted, "So it was really a terrific year except for the downside."

Question: What downside?

Ziegler: Watergate.

Lyn Nofziger, who served as a political adviser to Presidents Nixon and Reagan, was leaving the White House staff to go work for the Republican National Committee. "Now, Nofziger," said Nixon, "when you get to the National Committee, don't let them get away with a single lie."

"Mr. President," Nofziger replied, "I'm not even going to let them get away with the truth."

Nofziger later recalled that a week or two later, his answer popped up in the *New York Times*. Since he knew he hadn't planted it himself, he asked someone on the White House staff how his remark had got in the paper. The answer: "Well, the president was amused, and he went around telling it to everybody."

A few weeks after the assassination attempt on President Reagan in 1981, Nixon spoke to Nofziger: "Lyn, don't let the president make any decisions until he's completely well, because you don't make good decisions when you're sick. You know, I made the decision not to burn the [Watergate] tapes when I was recovering from pneumonia." As it turned out, Reagan did not heed the advice. When he was recovering from a colon cancer operation, he signed documents handed to him by Admiral John Poindexter to send missiles to Iran illegally.

Former congressman Donald Rumsfeld worked as an assistant to Nixon and later went on to serve in the Ford administration as Secretary of Defense and White House chief of staff. (These days he's back on familiar ground as Secretary of Defense in the

Bush II administration.) One day Nixon and George Shultz approached him and told him, "We want you to run the wage and price controls for the United States of America," referring to the Wage and Price Controls Board.

"But I don't believe in wage and price controls," Rumsfeld responded.

"We know," they replied. "That's why we want you to run them."

Herb Stein, Nixon's chairman of the Council of Economic Advisers, held a press conference to talk about the rising cost of food. He was going on and on about inflation being a case of too many dollars chasing too few goods and services, then concluded with a remark that left everyone a bit flummoxed: "What we've really discovered during this first peacetime experiment with wage and price controls in the history of the United States is that one of the last things that the American people are willing to give up is food."

At a luncheon for the White House press in 1972, Pat Nixon made it clear she was no pushover when it came to campaigning. She said that no one—not even her husband's advisers—told her what to do. "They often ask me for my advice," she said. "They find I have lots of experience."

She did say that if Nixon was reelected, he might make more historic trips abroad, such as the breakthrough trip to China. When asked if China's Chou En-lai would come to Washington, she laughed and said, "Well, that's it. We've got to be in the White House or he won't come."

She declined to answer only one question about Thomas Eagleton's withdrawal from the Democratic ticket: "I never comment on anyone's personal life and I don't want to be in the position of starting now."

* * *

It was a dubious moment in diplomatic history when President Nixon, attending the funeral of Charles de Gaulle, proclaimed, "This is a great day for France."

"You know, I've always wondered about the taping equipment. But I'm damn glad we have it." Nixon to H. R. Haldeman.

In the summer of 1974 and the waning days of the Nixon presidency, reporters accompanied Nixon on a trip to San Clemente, where his staff had decided to surprise him with a birthday cake. I was the designated pool reporter in Nixon's office when they wheeled it in, and Nixon stood up to read the inscription on the cake.

Then he stood back, and I noticed that icing from the cake had smeared all over his maroon blazer. Nixon's Irish setter, King Timahoe, hadn't missed the scene either, and wandered over and began licking the frosting off his master's coat as Nixon stood there with a frozen grin on his face.

In a note Tom Brokaw of NBC wrote me years later, he said, "I will never forget you describing for us, through tears of laughter, the utterly Nixon moment.... I believe it was the first time you were in a president's office without asking a question. There was nothing more to be said."

In September 2000, President Clinton attended a reception honoring Representative Eddie Bernice Johnson, a Texas Democrat, noting that they had known each other for twenty-eight years and had worked on the McGovern campaign in Texas in 1972:

"It was a pretty interesting experience. Senator McGovern got thirty-three [percent of the vote] in Texas. I never will forget, one day I was on a plane from Dallas to Little Rock with a young businessman from Jackson, Mississippi. He said, 'What are you doing?' And I told him what I was doing.

"He said, 'You're doing what?' I said, yes, I'm working for McGovern in Texas. And he looked at me and didn't crack a smile and said, 'You know, you're the only white man I ever met for McGovern.' It's a true story.

"Two years later, when Sam Ervin was having his [Watergate] hearings, the phone rang in my house in Little Rock one day, and it was this guy on the phone. He had kept my card and he said, 'I just called to tell you, you were right and I was wrong.'"

GERALD R. FORD

President Ford, without a doubt, had the best laugh of any president I've covered, and he wasn't afraid to use it. It came from down deep and he would throw his head back in genuine appreciation of a funny moment.

He had the good fortune to have people around who could make him laugh, and first and foremost was his wife, Betty. With her Midwestern sense of humor she was down-to-earth, honest, candid, and unafraid. She let the chips fall where they may and somehow had great faith in people. She knew they would understand Ford was not one to seize the moment for a one-liner. But then, he was not defensive, either.

He could take it on the chin—and he did, repeatedly, down flights of stairs—when the laugh was on him. But he was too kind to dish it out to his detractors.

He did not go out of his way to schmooze and win points with the opposition. He didn't have to—they trusted him. He had many friends among the Democrats while at the same time he maintained a strong sense of loyalty to his party and the country.

When he was sworn in as president, Ford said, "I am acutely aware that you have not elected me as your president by your ballots, so I ask you to confirm me with your prayers."

Ford also noted later, "It can go on and on, or someone must write 'The End' to it. I have concluded that only I can do that. And if

I can, I must, on announcing this pardon of Richard Nixon." On May 21, 2001, Ford's pardon of Nixon was seen in a twenty-five-year perspective and he was honored with the Profiles in Courage Award granted by the John F. Kennedy Foundation, for his political courage in an action that probably cost him the presidential election in 1976.

The award is named after Kennedy's Pulitzer Prize–winning book and is presented each year to an elected official who makes a principled decision in the face of strong political opposition.

"Because of that decision, which was differed with by great numbers of Americans, including myself, America was able to heal itself and move back to the path of reconciliation," Senator Edward Kennedy, brother of the late president, said at the award ceremony. "It was an extraordinary act of courage that historians recognize today was truly in the national interest."

But some of the familiar Gerry Ford came through as well in his acceptance speech when he thanked members of the Kennedy family and noted, "It is a very high honor, a very rare privilege for me to be here on this occasion. And I am deeply grateful to you, Caroline, the Kennedy family, for this award. History has been defined as argument without end.

"Come to think of it, Ted, much the same could be said of the United States Senate."

One of my all-time favorite stories about Ford occurred on the campaign trail when he and the press corps were walking down a street in Michigan and passed one of those old-fashioned "your weight and fortune" machines and the president decided to give it a shot.

He put in the coin and out popped a little card that he showed to everyone: "You are a brilliant leader. People listen to your opinions and you can wield great power."

After I read the card, I looked at Ford and said, "It got your weight wrong, too, Mr. President."

* * *

Betty Ford was one of the most stimulating first ladies ever, but her influence was more dramatically felt that autumn when she urged the president to make his most controversial decision, the pardon of Richard Nixon. She was one of several people who did, but I was later told that her opinion was a crucial factor in President Ford's final decision. She said, "I think it had to be done," and that the pardon "would be healing not only for the country but for the family as well, especially Mrs. Nixon."

At the National Press Club in September 1974, Ford attended the inauguration of the club's new president, Ronald Sarro of the *Washington Star News.* In his remarks Ford noted, "Anybody in public life is well aware of how important the judgments of the press are. I'm firmly convinced that if the good Lord had made the world today, He would have spent six days creating the heavens and earth and all the living creatures upon it. But on the seventh day He would not have rested. He would have had to justify it to Helen Thomas."

Betty Ford recalls in her memoirs, *Betty Ford: The Times of My Life,* that she went to the White House chief usher, Rex Scouten, and told him she felt "terribly uncomfortable here" and that when she spoke to the guards or the White House police, "they never answer me, just sort of back off." Next thing she knew Scouten had given orders to say "Good morning." She later found out that the Nixons had preferred more formality, "and the staff, trained to be as silent and invisible as possible, didn't know how to act with us." After a while, she said, everyone relaxed and "Jerry and the butler compared golf scores."

Not only was Betty candid but her children picked up Mom's habit as well. In August 1974, their son Jack was out West and told a reporter that his mother would be upset if Ford changed his mind and ran for president in 1976. Ford said later that he wished he'd been asked about that remark because "I'd have told them, 'Jack and I have a grand rapport and understanding, and I'm going to look after his mother and the White House and he's going to look after the bears and the tourists in Yellowstone.' "

Their son Mike, who was in Boston around the same time, was quoted as saying Richard Nixon owed the public "a total confession" of his part in Watergate. After what his father had been through with the pardon, Ford's reaction was pretty fatherly: "All my children have spoken for themselves since they first learned to speak, and not always with my advance approval. I expect that to continue."

Betty Ford handled a number of interviews her first few weeks in the White House and remarked to reporter Myra MacPherson that she had been asked nearly everything, except how often she sleeps with her husband.

"What would you have said?" asked MacPherson.

"As often as possible," said the first lady.

The first lady also caused quite a stir in an interview on *60 Minutes,* when she was asked what she would do if her daughter told her she was having an affair.

"Well, I wouldn't be a bit surprised," she said. "I think she's a perfectly normal human being like all girls. If she wanted to continue it, I would certainly counsel and advise her on the subject. And I'd want to know pretty much about the young man."

When President Ford was asked about his wife's remark, he said he thought he'd lost about 10 million votes. "Then when I read about it, I raised it to twenty million."

One of my favorite memories of Betty Ford's candor and forthright approach to life was from a moment in 1978. I was at the press center in Thurmont, Maryland, near Camp David, waiting for news about the Middle East peace negotiations and got a call from one of Gerald Ford's aides, telling me Betty was about to undergo some facial surgery.

When I asked if the procedure was cosmetic, the aide put the former first lady on the line.

"Are you going to have a face-lift?" I asked.

"Yes," she replied. "Isn't it wonderful? I'm sixty years old and I need a new face."

Traveling with a president is always some kind of adventure—and traveling with President Ford tended to have its more bizarre side.

UPI's Ron Cohen elected to go on two trips with the president, "the first when Squeaky Fromme tried to [assassinate] him in Sacramento," and a second trip to Hartford, Connecticut, when a carload of youths who had too much to drink sped into an intersection that the police had somehow neglected to block off. They managed to crash into a limo in Ford's motorcade. "Before the press car took off, I could see the occupants lying on the ground, with police and Secret Service standing over them with weapons," said Ron. "One can only guess what went flashing through their alcohol-impaired brains."

What made that Hartford incident even more strange was that it was probably the only time in history that a presidential limousine had been hit by another car—and it got hit twice. In such events, the Secret Service has one priority—get the president out. Thus, the lead car took off, and the presidential limousine took off, and the tail car took off. Then the lead car stopped, the presidential limousine smashed into the rear of the lead car, and the tail car bashed into the back of the limousine.

Ron said, "After those two incidents, I signed up for a third trip—a Ford speech in Charleston, West Virginia, which has one of the scarier airports in the world. [Press secretary] Ron Nessen called begging me not to come, and when I declined to reconsider, he specifically relegated me to the press plane, on the grounds that I was such bad luck that if a plane was going to crash with me on it, it wouldn't be Air Force One! Nothing untoward happened, of course, and I elected to quit wreaking havoc with the White House and resume doing it at [UPI headquarters] in Washington."

White House colleague Ira Allen had another close call in 1976, traveling with vice presidential candidate Bob Dole in Parkersburg, West Virginia: "When the plane landed with Dole aboard, there was no one but the advance team to meet him. When we returned to the airport, there was a fairly large crowd. I asked someone in the crowd what the occasion was and was told, 'Nobody's seen a plane this big ever take off from here.'"

I often marveled at Ford's sense of equanimity after two assassination attempts within weeks of each other in 1975. When flying back after the Squeaky Fromme incident, the pool reporters aboard Air Force One were still a little unsettled, and we imagined Ford would be, too, sitting quietly in his cabin. However, we were all wrong. Dennis Franey of the *Wall Street Journal* recalled in the book *The Flying White House,* "Somewhere over Indiana the president ambled back into a staff compartment in the middle of the plane, and it was immediately apparent he wasn't in a brooding mood at all. He was puffing contentedly on a pipe. He was smiling broadly. He was, it seemed, in the mood for a party."

It turned out he was. We had a round of drinks and told a lot of stories. Ron Nessen said Ford would recount the incident and his memories of it over and over again, even demonstrating how the Secret Service agents had doubled him over and hustled him away.

Seventeen days later, in San Francisco, Sara Jane Moore managed to fire a shot that narrowly missed Ford. After the Secret Service got him into the limousine and to the airport, Ford stopped before he boarded the presidential plane. He shook hands with the city police officers who had made up his motorcycle escort and ordered agent Ron Pontius to radio thanks to all the security personnel who'd protected him during the visit. Once he did board the plane, a steward was waiting for him with a frosty martini. Ford took a big gulp and grinned.

The rest of those aboard had a few drinks as well, as we waited for Betty Ford to arrive. She had been on the Monterey peninsula, and when she walked in, it became apparent she hadn't heard about the assassination attempt. "I watched her face intently to see what her reaction would be," Nessen recalled. "She never changed her expression. She just kept smiling and sipped her drink."

On the flight home, most of the White House staff were tense. Two assassination attempts in a little over two weeks? But Ford remained calm. He telephoned his daughter Susan and son Jack, enjoyed a steak dinner, and went to sleep.

When we arrived back in Washington, he made a brief appearance on television, praising San Francisco's hospitality and telling the public he intended to continue traveling around the country.

When he was asked why he would even want to take such risks after such close calls, Ford said, "The American people want a dialogue between them and their president. . . . And if we can't have that opportunity of talking with one another, seeing one another, shaking hands with one another, something has gone wrong in our society."

There was something about Ford and airplanes, though. Who can forget that overseas trip in March 1975 when Air Force One arrived in Salzburg, Austria, and he stumbled down the stairs in plain view of dignitaries, reporters, and most unfortunately, photographers? Later that day, the same thing happened at

Salzburg's Residenz Palace, where he was to meet with Egyptian President Anwar Sadat.

The press corps began hounding Nessen: Was something wrong with the president? In later years, Nessen attributed the apparent clumsiness to Ford's not getting proper rest on an uncomfortable bed in Madrid and "fatigue, compounding the usual stiffness in his knees from old football injuries." But the image stuck for years.

Sometimes the press is appreciated—not often, but sometimes. On the campaign trail with President Ford in 1976, Ford's pardon of Nixon after the Watergate scandal seemed to be a sore point with people who turned out at events. I remember running with the "thundering herd" of reporters and photographers into a hall in Bad Axe, Michigan, to hear Ford give his stump speech. A man stopped me and said, "You saved the country." I was a little taken aback by that. Of course, he meant the press that had pursued the truth about Watergate and put a halt to the scandal in the Nixon White House.

At the 1997 rededication of his presidential library in Grand Rapids, Michigan, Ford invited former Presidents Jimmy Carter and George Bush to join him on the podium. Ford effusively praised Carter's humanitarian works and noted that his ventures and adventures are so global, he must live on an airplane. President Bush, he also noted, liked to jump out of airplanes, as he did that year. Ford went on to say that Bush had invited him along on the skydiving expedition and, mimicking comedian Dana Carvey's imitation of Bush, said, "Not gonna do it. Wouldn't be prudent." Besides, added Ford, "after all those jokes about my golf swing, do you really want to tempt fate by having me jump out an airplane?"

*   *   *

I think Ford has been one of the rare few who have realized how humor is the great leaven for presidents. At the 1975 Gridiron dinner, his remarks included the following:

"I've learned how much of a lifesaving medicine a little laughter is for presidents. So if a fine evening of fun and friendship like this is good for presidents, it must also be good for America.

"The Gridiron Club nurtures this great national asset. And I'm very glad we can all poke gentle jokes at ourselves and one another just this way—singeing without really burning—and I hope it will always stay that way.

"Americans are a very diverse people, living together in many different styles and many different places. We are united more by the way we look at things than by the traditional ties of blood or belief or battles long forgotten. And when we are able to look at the brighter side of our troubles, and the lighter side of our struggles, and see the smile that lies just below the surface of our neighbor's face, I think we Americans are at our very best."

Ford and Soviet leader Leonid Brezhnev were meeting in Vladivostok for arms reduction talks. Brezhnev had given Ford a wood representation of what was said to be Ford's likeness. The artwork was made up of many different pieces and different varieties of wood, carefully arranged. Ford came out of the meeting and showed the artwork to members of his staff. He wanted to make sure that Brezhnev's gift made an impression. As he was displaying it, White House photographer David Kennerly piped up, "Hey, that's great! Who is it? Frank Sinatra?"

During the 1976 presidential campaign, one of the big issues was Ford's pardon of Richard Nixon after Watergate. Ford has always said he believed he had done the right thing, but in campaign mode, he wasn't exactly eager to dwell on it. At a presidential news conference, journalist Fred Barnes of *The New*

Republic asked, "Mr. President, two or three times today you talked about your 'predecessor,' and you once referred to 'Lyndon Johnson's successor.' Are you trying to avoid saying the name Richard M. Nixon?"

Ford's answer was simple and to the point: "Yes."

Secretary of State Henry Kissinger continued to conduct his world-famous "shuttle diplomacy" in the Ford White House. On one of Kissinger's many missions to the Middle East, my former UPI colleague Dick Growald was aboard the plane flying to Damascus. The chief of Kissinger's Secret Service detail went back to the galley to get some food. An Uzi submachine gun was sitting on top of a box of bread, and the agent picked it up to get at the bread. Suddenly the plane dipped and the Uzi slipped out of his hands. Apparently, the safety was off, and when the gun hit the floor, it fired a round. No damage was done, but the agent, realizing he could have killed someone, fainted.

When he came to, Kissinger was standing over him and demanded, "Why didn't you tell me you wanted off the detail?" Then the secretary turned to the rest of the entourage. "Can you believe it? I'm the only man in the world who would have a bodyguard who would decide to shoot himself with a submachine gun at a distance of six inches. And miss."

In 1976, Dick Cheney worked for Ford as his chief of staff, and the spring brought some of the hardest-fought primary contests they had ever encountered. Ford had taken New Hampshire in February and captured Florida and Illinois, but Reagan won in South Carolina. The race was getting to a point where every single delegate vote counted, so the Ford team launched a massive effort to secure each one. People would be flown in to Washington for briefings, to the White House for cocktails with the president, anything to convince them to commit their votes.

One Republican delegate, Cheney said, "used to change sides

each week. But we brought her down to the White House repeatedly, and the president finally closed the deal when we brought in about forty of her relatives. He took them into the Oval Office and met with them for about two hours—all for one vote. That was how hard we worked for those delegates."

In the midst of all these exhausting efforts, one night a man jumped the fence outside the White House while the first family was inside. He went charging toward the mansion brandishing a large pipe. The police officer on duty shouted for the man to stop, but he kept on going. The officer then fired a warning shot, and when the intruder kept making his way toward the White House, the officer took aim and shot him on the spot.

Of course, all hell broke loose. The officer, who had been on the force for a short time, was understandably shaken by it all, so he was brought to the Secret Service post under the West Wing of the White House.

As he sat there, trying to calm down, one of his colleagues came up to him, put a hand on the officer's shoulder, and said, "You know, we're going to be in an awful lot of trouble with the president if that guy you shot was an uncommitted delegate."

At the 1976 convention, Ford selected Senator Bob Dole of Kansas to be his running mate, and afterward the president and Dole decided it would be a good thing to travel to Dole's hometown of Russell, Kansas, after the convention and hold a rally. This did not go over well with the staff, which had been working twenty-four-hour days for weeks on end and was looking forward to a little time off before the fall campaign got into full swing. Cheney explained to the president that if they went ahead with that plan, it would have to be a first-class event, since it would be the first official stop after the nomination. But Ford was not to be deterred.

So the staff went into overdrive, buying radio time all over the western part of the state to publicize the rally, arranging travel via bus (Russell had no airport), setting up security, making all the necessary preparations.

Ford flew in aboard Air Force One to the nearest airport, about fifty miles away, and then took a helicopter to Russell.

As a result of the hard work of an extremely exhausted staff, the place was packed. Taking a look around him, Ford tapped Cheney on the knee and said, "You see, I knew we'd get a crowd."

On that little jaunt, Ford and his entourage pulled up in front of the modest home where Dole's mother lived to pay her a visit. Unfortunately, she wasn't home. Like everyone else, she had headed off for the Ford-Dole rally in town.

I think Ford's acceptance speech for the Profiles in Courage Award probably best typifies how he should be remembered:

"It's a very high honor and a great privilege for me to be here and particularly to be the recipient of one of the Profiles in Courage Awards," Ford said before the ceremony. He said he had pardoned Nixon to heal the country, which was bitterly divided over the Vietnam War, and because Nixon's misdeeds were a distraction.

"When I became president, the country was in total turmoil with the war in Vietnam and the Watergate scandals. It was important to try to heal the wounds of those two tragedies," Ford said. "I should have been spending, in that first month, one hundred percent of my time on the problems of the country. The only way to clear the desk in the Oval Office was to get Mr. Nixon's problems off my agenda and get my total attention on the problems of the country."

In his speech later, he noted, "In the course of almost eighty-eight years, I've seen more than my share of miracles. I have witnessed the defeat of Nazi tyranny, the destruction of hateful walls that once divided free men from the enslaved. . . . My generation has celebrated the end of polio, cheered as men left their footprints on the moon, and scratched its head while trying to figure out the difference between a gigabyte and a Happy Meal.

"None of this just happened. It happened because people of conscience refused to be passive in the face of injustice or indifferent to the demands of democracy. Now a new generation in a new century is summoned to complete our unfinished work and to purge our politics of cynicism. Today the challenge of political courage looms larger than ever before. Our political life is becoming so expensive, so mechanized, and so dominated by professional politicians and public relations men that the idealist who dreams of independent statesmanship is rudely awakened by the necessity of the election and accomplishments. So said Senator John Kennedy in introducing *Profiles in Courage*. Forty-five years later, his concerns are more relevant than ever.

"If there is distrust out there—and, unfortunately, there is—perhaps it is because there is so much partisan jockeying for advantage at the expense of public policy. At times, it feels as if the American politics consists largely of candidates without ideals hiring consultants without conviction to stage campaigns without concern. Increasingly, the result is elections without voters.

"It doesn't have to be that way. Wherever I go on my various travels around the country, I sense a longing for community and a desire on the part of Americans to be part of something bigger, finer than themselves."

JIMMY CARTER

Jimmy Carter promised the American people, "I'll never lie to you." He also said, "I'm not a very good joke-teller." In fact, he would often have to rely on the legendary sense of humor of his mother, Miss Lillian, when he chose to lighten the moment. He liked to tell of the reporter who ran up to Miss Lillian after the election results in 1976 declared him the winner. "Aren't you proud of your son?" the reporter asked. "Which one?" she said. Not to mention how, when Carter told Miss Lillian he was going to run for president, she asked him, "Of what?"

If I wanted a laugh on the White House detail in Plains, Georgia, I would head over for a visit with Miss Lillian or to see brother Billy. The president had made much of the fact that he was born-again, and one day I asked Billy if he, too, was born-again. "Once is enough," he answered.

President Carter must miss the sunshine they brought into his life—his mother and siblings, who knew that life had its lighter moments.

When we think of the Carter presidency, we really get serious—even pious. Not necessarily funny. He did have a witty side to him but kept it out of the way for the most part, and at times a bitterness overcame him, not unlike Richard Nixon's view—a feeling he was not accepted on his own terms. (Southern presidents have had that hang-up—maybe with some justification in the Northeast.)

But he has been the most humanitarian past president we have known in the last half of the twentieth century. Christianity was and is a large part of Carter's life, but he never tried to inflict it on others. His administration might have been short on laughs, but his sense of duty and public service make him long on stature.

In his announcement for the presidency in December 1974, Carter said, "It is time to ask ourselves what our commanding officer, Admiral Hyman Rickover, asked me and every other officer who served with him in an atomic submarine: 'For our nation, for all of us, that question is "Why Not the Best?" ' "

After speaking to a Democratic gathering in 1975, Carter was asked about Betty Ford's reply in an interview that she would not be a bit surprised if her daughter had an affair. Carter responded that he and his wife would be "deeply hurt, shocked, and disappointed . . . because our daughter is only seven years old."

In 1975, Bill Cotterell says, "I don't remember who it was, but one Northeast reporter wrote a profile of Jimmy and Rosalynn and had them strolling hand in hand beneath their peanut trees. Of course, it was a pecan orchard near their property, but Carter staffers let the guy believe peanuts grow on trees. City folks, I'll tell ya . . ."

On the campaign trail in Ohio in May 1976, Carter mistakenly shook the hand of a department store mannequin. "Better give her a brochure, too," he quipped.

When asked why there was such an age gap between their young daughter, Amy, and her older brothers, Carter said, "My wife and I had an argument for fourteen years, which I finally won."

In 1976, Carter found a way to defuse all the cracks about his wide and toothy grin. At a speech he told the audience, "My tax return is coming out okay. The only thing the IRS questioned was a six-hundred-dollar bill for toothpaste."

On the campaign trail with Carter in 1976, UPI White House reporter Ira Allen said the airport in Charleston, West Virginia, "gave me the worst, well, make it second-worst, scare of my flying experience. Carter had spoken in Charleston, and when we got to the airport—which is something like a leveled-off mountaintop—it was fogged in. So we sat in the plane and waited and waited. Finally, after a half hour or so, the pilot of the charter said he was going to spin the plane around and let the jets blow away the fog long enough to get clearance to take off. And that's what he did, as everyone sat white-knuckled."

After the 1976 election, White House aide Jody Powell called Joe Laitin and asked him to spend an evening brainstorming because he'd heard so much about Joe. The night they got together, Jody said, "I had a nightmare. I dreamed Jimmy had been killed." Joe replied, "Only vice presidents are supposed to have dreams like that, not press secretaries."

Talk about lusting in your heart for a whole country: It was strange enough when, during the presidential debate between Gerald Ford and Jimmy Carter, Ford said Poland was not under Soviet domination. But something really got lost in the translation when, in a speech in Poland in 1977, it was reported that Carter said, "I desire the Poles carnally."

When Carter decided to run for president, let it not be said his modesty was not in check. Dick Taffe, who worked in UPI's Boston bureau, recalled the day Carter arrived in the bureau "sans entourage, except for press secretary Jody Powell—who we initially mistook for the Georgia governor because the 'other guy' was carrying his own coat bag."

The two had walked in unannounced and introduced them-selves. Unfortunately, no one had time to interview Carter. So staffer Jim Wieck called Dave Rosen over from the statehouse, and he spent an hour or two with the would-be president. Afterward, Jim asked Dave how it went. "This guy is good," said Dave. "He could win it."

Dave, now a vice president at Emerson College, later said, "I remember the incident well, although I am surprised to hear I was smart enough to know Carter could actually win. Powell put together a press conference for Carter at the statehouse, and it was sparsely attended. An uncle of mine from a small town in New York happened to be visiting me that day, and he came to the press conference. He talked about it for months to come, espe-cially after Carter was elected."

Early on in Carter's presidential bid, I tried to cover a Bible study class that he taught in Plains, Georgia. All of the male reporters were allowed in, but when I tried to enter, a man standing at the door blocked my way and told me ladies were not allowed in.

"I'm no lady, I'm a reporter," I told him, and he stepped aside for me.

Bill Cotterell, who covered Carter in Georgia, recalled that some Carter staffers used to keep mementos of what could be referred to as the "wilderness years." "I remember seeing several clippings in the press office from Arizona and Oregon, et cetera, referring to him as an 'Alabama governor,' 'Georgia senator,' 'Georgia governor [not "former"],' Mississippi this-or-that, and even one story that began, 'Southern leader Jimmy Carter came to town Tuesday and said . . .' It seemed like some reporter had done an impromptu interview and later wondered, 'Oh, jeez, who was that guy?'"

*   *   *

But it seemed Carter was in the wilderness even in Georgia now and then. He told a great story in August 1973 to the Georgia Association of Colleges:

"Early one morning, immediately following my campaign, when I made my first foray into the rest of Georgia after becoming governor, I went into a restaurant in southwest Georgia and I asked for an order of hotcakes, and the girl in there brought me one little piece of butter. After I had finished about half the hotcakes, I called her over and I told her that if she didn't mind, I'd like to have some more butter.

"She turned around and walked away and said, 'No.' I figured she didn't understand what I meant, so the next time she came by, which was quite a while later, I said, 'Young lady, would you come over here a minute please; I'd like to have another pat of butter.' And she said, 'No,' and left again.

"Finally, I asked the security man who was with me to go get her and bring her back. When she walked over, I said, 'Listen, I don't want to make an issue of this, but I want some more butter.' She said, 'You're not going to have it.'

"I said, 'Do you know who I am?'

"She said, 'Who?'

"I said, 'I'm the governor of Georgia.'

"She said, 'Do you know who I am?'

"I said, 'No.'

"She said, 'I'm the keeper of the butter.'"

At the 1976 Democratic National Convention, Bill Cotterell was trying to make polite cocktail chatter with a Minnesota delegate who thought the ticket was upside down—that Mondale should have been on top and (just maybe) Carter was fit to be vice president.

"She was asking me a lot about this odd Georgian I'd covered," he said. "I noticed she had a large lapel button that said TANSTAAFL, which I took to be some Scandinavian name. Trying to be polite, I was just about to say something about how the Carter staff thought highly of her guy—wasn't he a congressman? Mayor of Lake Wobegon? But something held me back, so I asked her who Tanstaafl was.

" 'There ain't no such thing as a free lunch,' she replied."

Bill Cotterell also recalled that he was driving from Atlanta to Plains the morning after Carter won the New Jersey, Ohio, and California primaries, wrapping it all up. A country music station, he said, led off its morning news this way:

"Americus police report no calls overnight. . . . There was a small fire in the back of Gibson's Groceries . . . and a Sumter County man will be the Democratic nominee for president. Details after this."

When Carter was in the White House, Jody Powell was invited to speak at a Georgia Democratic Party dinner at the northeast Georgia town of Elberton with the state House Speaker, Tom Murphy, who had loathed Carter as governor.

Murphy offered Bill Cotterell and Jody a lift back to Atlanta on a state plane. Once they were airborne, however, Murphy insisted that the plane fly over Atlanta and drop him at Bremen (over on the Alabama border), then double back and take Bill and Jody to the airport. Bill recalled that he didn't care "since I was just going home, but Powell needed to get back to Washington. He told me later he thought Murphy was getting even with Carter one more time. So when we got to Murphy's Haralson County, we had to circle for a half hour because the sheriff said there were cows on the runway. Murphy seemed to enjoy that. I bet Powell didn't get home before sunrise."

Jody Powell used to say that Carter was "tight as a tick" about money, and when Jody asked Joe Laitin for any advice once the Carter administration was moving into the White House, Joe told him to be sure to hang on to Connie Gerrard, who had kept the press office running through five administrations.

At the time, Connie was making $25,000 a year, and Powell, a little negative, asked, "Do you realize how much money she makes?"

"I don't know, but it's not enough," said Joe.

From Bill Cotterell: When Carter was governor in 1974, he hosted a meeting of the Commission on the Future of the South, a group of academics and government leaders, up in the extreme north Georgia mountains at a state-owned resort called Unicoi Station. During this meeting, which drew a lot of national press looking at this novelty Southern governor, Carter held a news conference about many political topics. He was also chairman of a DNC campaign committee raising some money at the time.

The race for governor that year featured Lieutenant Governor Lester Maddox, a segregationist who had preceded Carter as governor, and Carter certainly didn't want him returning to the governor's mansion. Maddox and Carter couldn't stand each other, and it would have embarrassed Carter's presidential campaign to have Maddox sniping at him with the credibility of the governor's office. Carter backed Bert Lance, who later became his budget chief in the White House.

During a news conference, I asked Carter if it would "embarrass" Georgia if Maddox was returned to the mansion. Carter replied blandly that Georgia was bigger than any one man or any one administration and would survive, but he thought it would be better if Lance went to the Capitol's second floor for four years. Afterward, as the press was packing up, Jody came over to me and said the governor wanted to see me, off the record.

"When you asked me if the state would be embarrassed by electing Lester," Carter said, after reascertaining that we were off the record, "all I could think of was, how do you embarrass a state that four times elected Gene Talmadge?"

(Herman Talmadge, Gene's son, was reelected to the U.S. Senate that year. Bert Lance lost to state Representative George Busbee, who beat Maddox in the Democratic runoff. Busbee was no friend of Carter's but was preferable to Maddox in Carter's view.)

Carter used to fly into Dobbins Air Force Base north of Atlanta on Air Force One when he was president. Bill Cotterell would be sent out from the Atlanta bureau to log in the plane, keeping a line open to Washington so I could dash for the press pool car. I'd hand him my copy that I'd written on the plane, shout a few instructions if we needed something else, and dash off again.

Usually, they rolled a flatbed truck out for the press to stand on. For safety, there'd be a waist-high railing. Bill would put his phone on the T-shaped joint formed by the railing and a vertical post so as to easily dictate the copy to Washington. One day he was at his usual post, dictating the scene—"Now Carter is shaking hands with the mayor, now Rosalynn is greeting some children"—that sort of thing.

"I felt what I thought was a breeze ruffling my trouser cuffs, but it persisted. I looked down and Hamilton Jordan had untied my shoelaces and was tying them together on the far side of the fence post. I was glad I'd caught him, so I didn't try to walk away when the motorcade left. I forgot I was on the phone and leaned down to shake hands with Jordan. The dictationist in Washington kind of panicked because of my prolonged silence, maybe envisioning another Dallas. When I put the phone back to my ear, she was shouting, 'What's happening now? What's happening?'

" 'Well,' I said with as much dignity as I could muster, 'I had to stop because the White House chief of staff tied my shoelaces together. . . . Oh, never mind, where was I . . .' "

At the White House Correspondents Association dinner in 1977, people were simultaneously chuckling over Carter's after-dinner speech and wondering if anyone had written it for him. Speculation ran from White House personnel director Jim King, who denied it, to speechwriter Jerry Doolittle. In any case, it was a Carter we didn't see often.

"I've had a lot of setbacks, as you know, and you've been kind enough to make those clear," Carter told the crowd. "And I want you to know I have instructed my press secretary, Jody Powell, to find out who at the White House used the phrase 'cruel recluse' to describe me. Jody is now interrogating everyone at the White House, including twenty-three staff members, so I'll be letting you know when we find out who said it. If not, my new press secretary will."

Carter had also taken a lot of criticism for not appointing more women and minorities to high administration posts. He looked around at the dais, with nearly all white men sitting there, and commented, "Of course, I have derived a lot of inspiration from looking at this head table tonight."

At the spring 1977 Gridiron dinner, it was close to a draw with Carter and Walter Mondale as to who from the administration got the best laughs.

The curtain rose on Carter troops bearing suit-hanger bags over the right shoulder, in the new presidential style, and singing to the tune of "Marching Through Georgia," with the chorus:

> Repent, repent, you Yankees don't forget
> We won, we won, you ain't seen nothin' yet:
> We give all the orders now, and you'll like what you get.
> Now we are marching from Georgia.

Senate Majority Leader Howard Baker of Tennessee got a laugh when he said that President Carter had originally planned to appoint Billy Carter head of the CIA, but Billy didn't want to be head of anything he couldn't spell.

The president did not arrive until after Baker's turn at the podium, but was in time to hear some funny lines from Vice President Mondale, who, according to many, was hilarious. When he poked fun at Carter's foreign policy, the president laughed as much as anyone.

"There are big changes in this administration's foreign policy compared to the last," said Mondale. "In the Ford administration they held daily foreign policy briefings—whereas we have a daily foreign policy.

"I go to Paris, I go to Rome, and he goes to Plains, Georgia, and Clinton, Massachusetts," Mondale said. He also boasted about how he got better treatment than his boss. "On Inauguration Day I rode from the Capitol to the White House in a chauffeured limousine. The president had to walk. Whenever I take a trip, aides carry my luggage. The president carries his own."

Carter made sure his face was like stone when it was his turn to speak, and he referred to Mondale as "the acting vice president of the United States."

He told the audience he had heard all the cracks about his foreign policy being disastrous, but he thought there "should be some continuity from the last administration" to his. And on a serious note, he said, "In every instance that I have known of with confrontation with the government and the press, the press was always right. So keep it up."

S. I. Hayakawa, the new Democratic senator from California that year, took a ribbing as well. A columnist dressed in a karate suit lead a choir in which the familiar Hallelujah Chorus by Handel was transformed into a "Hayakawa" chorus to herald his arrival.

Naturally, several in the audience turned to see how the real-life senator was taking it. He was taking it fine. He was asleep.

June 1978: A few hundred tourists at the Lincoln Memorial were treated to an unexpected sight-seeing bonus late at night, when President Carter decided to take visiting Prime Minister Morarji Desai of India on a quick tour of the shrine.

The White House didn't mention the impromptu fifteen-minute visit, made about 9:40 P.M. Tom Thornton, a staff member of the National Security Council, said Carter reported he had never been confronted with so many popping flash-bulbs as when he and Desai had walked down the steps of the Memorial.

Carter seemed to have a good time at the 1978 Gridiron dinner when he and Rosalynn teamed up and wowed the audience with their jitterbugging to the tune of "Sweet Georgia Brown." Allan Cromley of the *Daily Oklahoman* was Gridiron president that year and had seen the Carters dance at a White House reception. He had suggested to White House aides that the first couple might want to do a number at the Gridiron. Mrs. Carter was okay with the idea, but the president, while not rejecting it outright, never gave an affirmative answer. Right up to the last minute, Cromley wasn't sure what they would do. But when he gave the signal to go onstage, the president followed the first lady and seemed pleased with the uproarious reaction from the audience.

Carter declined to attend the next two Gridiron events, but Mrs. Carter made a bit of history in 1979 when she attended and delivered the speech for the Democrats.

"Nothing would have kept Jimmy away except matters of most urgent national importance," she said. "As you know, he had to go to Elk City, Oklahoma."

From UPI audio reporter Tom Foty, on one of those familiar softball games in Georgia:

"During the Fourth of July weekend in 1980, Carter took time out from the campaign to go back home and played in one of those games in Plains, Georgia. Bill [Cotterell] is right that the Carter team had a definite conditioning advantage, made up mostly of Secret Service types. I was playing first base for the press side and was reaching for an infield throw after Carter hit a grounder or liner.

"Watching for the throw, not the runner, I barely caught him in the corner of my eye bearing down on me at full gallop, his face in a full clinch.

"Sure enough, he bumped into me, more or less knocking me over. All this was captured by some network cameras, so a couple of the evening newscasts that night featured footage of the president knocking over a guy in a colorful yellow softball shirt . . . with a very prominent UPI logo on it.

"Recognizing the shirt from games on the Mall, some UPI Washington staffers later told me they were wondering who that was. But Carter was not going to give an inch on that play or any other. While on the pitcher's mound, his facial expressions looked like Randy Johnson in the play-offs.

"I still have that yellow UPI shirt and an autographed picture of Carter from the game with Larry McQuillen, Helen Thomas, and yours truly watching him near the batter's cage."

At the 1980 Democratic National Convention, Carter left some scratching their heads and wondering what century he was talking about when he said, "I am speaking of a great man who should have been president and would have been one of the greatest presidents in history—Hubert Horatio Hornblower."

After Carter lost the 1980 election, the press corps decided to give him a farewell dinner. After a few obligatory remarks, he ended his speech by saying, "I want to thank all of you who made my job so easy and enjoyable and comfortable."

Then he turned to his wife and said, "Thank you, Rosalynn."

* * *

When Carter turned seventy-five, I was honored to be one of the guests at a huge celebration at the Rylander Theater in Americus, Georgia, in October 1999.

"I'm glad I made it," he told the audience. "As far as my mental capacity and my physical capacity, I've never had a better time in my life." Of his loss to Ronald Reagan in 1980, he said, "At that time, I looked on it as an embarrassing failure. I could rationalize and say, 'If the hostages hadn't been held, I would have been reelected,'" referring to the 1979 takeover of the U.S. embassy in Iran, when Iranian students held fifty-two Americans hostage for more than a year. "I had a lot of unfulfilled expectations."

But he has gone on to much greater things and is perhaps the most active ex-president around (the jury is still out on Bill Clinton).

"I've had ups and downs," Carter said, "but almost invariably the downs have become some of the most fortunate things in my life."

Jimmy Carter has written a lot of books and he's in a position to offer a little advice now and then. In January 2001, Carter and Secretary of State Madeleine Albright were appearing on ABC's *Good Morning America*. Albright, who had just finished being interviewed by Charles Gibson, spotted Carter, who was just about to sit for his interview with Diane Sawyer.

After a quick hug and a kiss, Albright told Carter of her plan to write a book. "So," she said, "how do you write those books so fast?"

"I get up early," replied Carter.

RONALD REAGAN

What can I say that hasn't already been said? Many have tried, but so far no one has been able to take the title The Great Communicator away from Ronald Reagan. He's the winner and still champ.

Self-deprecation was his stock-in-trade, and his timing skills had been honed for years before a camera—even his comparing himself to Methuselah was funny. He loved to tell stories that amplified his sense of optimism and patriotism, and any anecdote to knock the size of the federal government.

Government was being run by bureaucrats on the Potomac, he would say in so many ways. But he brought in more than a few of his own, and they stayed long after he had left.

Age and big government were his mainstays for humorous opening lines and a good way to win over audiences.

He liked to tell jokes about his Hollywood days, but he also had a reassuring way with a wisecrack. When a would-be assassin took a shot at him in March 1981, his remark to his wife, Nancy—"Honey, I forgot to duck"—and his comment to the doctors when he was being taken to surgery—"I hope you're all Republicans"—helped the nation breathe just a little easier.

His sense of humor reinforced his Mr. Nice Guy image even when his administration was declaring ketchup a vegetable in school lunch programs and violating congressional mandates about selling arms to Iran.

He had a way of putting people at ease with his gentle—

sometimes not so gentle—gibes, and his comic timing served him well when he would turn the joke on himself, as he did more often than not.

Many did not care for what he said—but there's no doubt that nearly everyone loved the way he said it. Gerald Ford once noted, "He was one of the few political leaders I have ever met whose public speeches revealed more than his private conversations."

All the stories about Nancy Reagan's influence on her husband might have got an early start when Reagan started holding news conferences. Nancy is reported to have held his hand before each one and instructed him, "When Helen Thomas says, 'Thank you, Mr. President,' you leave."

From Art McGuinn in San Francisco: "Best shot I saw about a candidate's appearance was from Bob Dole, who said he didn't believe Reagan dyed his hair, he was just 'prematurely orange.'

"When Reagan was governor, a photographer and I surprised him in the barbershop of the Senator Hotel in Sacramento to inspect the gubernatorial mane and report results for the public benefit. Neither of us could see any gray, and the hotel barber, his weekly regular—no fancy stuff for him at that time—said he did not dye his hair. Ronnie was quite game about the matter."

After his debate with Jimmy Carter, Reagan was asked whether he had been nervous. "No," he said, "I've been on the same stage with John Wayne."

In 1980 a river navigation project was in the works to link the Tennessee River with the Gulf of Mexico via the Tombigbee River, which runs down the Alabama-Mississippi border. Nancy Reagan, who was campaigning for her husband in Mississippi, was asked by a voter at a rally, "What do you think of Tennessee-Tombigbee?"

"I don't think I've had the pleasure of meeting Mr. Bigbee," she replied.

He thinks that he will never see . . . President Reagan on vegetation:

"A tree's a tree. How many more do you need to look at?"

"When you've seen one redwood, you've seen them all."

"I don't believe a tree is a tree and if you've seen one, you've seen them all."

Soon after the 1980 election, I asked Mrs. Reagan what her project in the White House would be. "I don't have one," she said. "My husband is most important." She went on to say that she would concentrate on her husband and her home.

"You will make a big mistake if you don't pursue some great goal," I warned her. "You will have the help of a big staff, so don't miss the chance to do some great good that will go down in the history books."

For some time, I guess, she chose to ignore my advice and spent her time redecorating the private quarters, acquiring new china, and planning elegant White House entertainments. When I was asked later, I noted that I wasn't too surprised to see her running into trouble with the media.

Jokes about Reagan's work habits permeated eight years of his presidency, and he, as usual, turned them into fodder for his own remarks. Perhaps one of the best was at a White House Correspondents Association dinner when he told the crowd he'd been working really hard, "burning the midday oil."

Of the many new White House staffers who arrived with the Reagan administration, press secretary Jim Brady was one of the best. He was well regarded and respected by the press corps, and, likewise, largely treated reporters and photographers with respect. His banter sometimes equaled that of his boss, as he once referred to his job, partly in humor, as "the second most challenging job in the free world." When Reagan appointed him, the balding, avuncular Brady told reporters, "I come before you today as not just another pretty face but out of sheer talent."

His nickname was Bear, and he was often seen sporting a big brown button that said "Bear with Me."

One daily briefing seemed to contain far fewer answers than questions, and he joked, "I've gotten so bad on giving out information that the IRS has promulgated a new ruling. Lunches with me as a source are no longer deductible."

In those all-too-familiar budget battles with Congress, Reagan somehow always managed to win the war, despite the Democrat-controlled Congress. At a fund-raising reception in Ohio in November 1981, Reagan took a shot at the partisan skirmishes: "Speaker [Tip] O'Neill says that I know less about the budget than any president he's ever known. Well, maybe we're not talking about the same kind of budgets. I presided over eight balanced budgets as governor of California, and he's only seen a balanced budget once in his twenty-seven years in Congress. And I could point out that since I became president, there hasn't been a federal budget for me to look at."

On a trip to China, Reagan made a speech on Chinese television. However, the Chinese government didn't want the Chinese people to hear everything he had to say and blocked out some parts of his address. We in the press corps came rushing over afterward to get his reaction. How was he going to stand for such censorship? How could he allow this to happen—his full message not getting through to the Chinese people?

Reagan just smiled at all of us and replied, "Oh, it didn't bother me at all. You guys do it all the time."

* * *

While Reagan was the most skillful presidential communicator since FDR, he could also be guilty of a blooper or two. At a Rose Garden ceremony for Liberian head of state Samuel K. Doe, Reagan referred to his guest as "Chairman Moe."

During a 1982 state dinner in Brazil, Reagan drank a toast to Bolivia, then explained his flub by saying that was his next stop. The next morning, he flew off to Colombia.

Introducing comedian Bob Hope at a banquet one year, Reagan noted that Hope "has two great loves. He loves to entertain and he loves golf. Just the other day he asked me, 'What's your handicap?' And I said, 'Congress.'"

One of Reagan's goals in his presidency was to see an end to communism. At his summit with Soviet leader Mikhail Gorbachev in Geneva, Reagan told him a joke: An American and a Soviet citizen were comparing their forms of government. The American said, "I can walk into the Oval Office and I can slam my fist down on the desk, and I can say that I don't like the way Ronald Reagan is running the United States."

"Well," the Soviet replied, "I can do the same thing in the Politburo. I can go into Gorbachev's office and slam my fist on his desk and say that I don't like the way Ronald Reagan is running the United States."

In October 1983, Reagan addressed the Heritage Foundation at its tenth anniversary celebration: "It's wonderful for Nancy and me to be here tonight and see old friends like Joe Coors of the Coors Brewing family. Actually, I was a little surprised by the warmth of Joe's introduction. I'm not sure how many of you know this, but there's a certain coolness between Joe and me tonight. I guess maybe that's my fault. When I arrived at the reception here, I said, 'Joe, it's been a long, hard day in the Oval Office, but now it's Miller time.' That's when he showed me his Mondale button.

"Seriously, though, where are those Democratic candidates with their grandiose solutions now that we need them? The America's Cup race, for example. Now, there was a problem that could have been solved with more money and a lot of wind."

At the annual Salute to Congress dinner in February 1981, sponsored by the Washington Press Club Foundation, Reagan not only got a chance to salute his wife but also managed to poke fun yet again at his age and the women of Washington's press corps. "I'm a little surprised to find myself at this podium tonight," he began. "I know your organization was founded by six Washington newspaperwomen in 1919—seems only yesterday.

"I know that it was Washington's National Press Club for over a half a century, so I thought that tonight's production would be equal time, right? A night for Nancy. Then I learned of your 1971 pioneering and coeducational Washington press corps. You changed the name. You admitted male members. You also encouraged male speakers.

"So, here I am, a poor but modest substitute for the former Nancy Davis, ready to defend myself and every other middle-aged male in America I can define as 'middle-aged.' That's when you're faced with two temptations and you choose the one that'll get you home at nine o'clock.

"I do want to congratulate the Washington Press Club for forward-looking leadership, and I hope that Ann McFeatters and Carol Richards and all of you succeed quickly in your effort to acquire a clubhouse. And if we have our way and you wait a little bit, there will be several public buildings that will be open to you.

"But to get back to the view of the press club, I think that you're taking this honeymoon idea too seriously. I passed a Marriott drive-in and saw Helen Thomas trying to carry [White

House press secretary] Jim Brady over the threshold. But it isn't all honeymoon. If I'm on a honeymoon, romance is dead in Washington. Jesse Helms wants me to move to the right; Lowell Weicker wants me to move to the left; Teddy Kennedy wants me to move back to California. And while I have the opportunity with so many of the press, I want you to know that it is not true that the Moral Majority has been trying to exert undue influence. That rumor started recently when Jerry Falwell called me with a suggestion for ambassador to Iran: the publisher of *Penthouse*.

"I've been spending some of my time trying to meet the Democratic members of Congress halfway, and the halfway house I found is Tip O'Neill's office."

There was a bit of consternation among the press corps in August 1981 regarding Libya's harassment of U.S. planes in international airspace. After a skirmish at sea, Reagan's advisers decided not to wake him to tell him what had happened. He addressed the situation in Costa Mesa, California, at a fundraising event with Orange County Republicans:

"Now, we were aware that there might be some harassment, because for the last couple of years, Libyan planes have come out and harassed not only our planes out in international waters, but French planes, and in one instance or two have even fired. Whether they were firing directly at the plane or not, we don't know, but this was the kind of harassment tactics they were following. And in the briefing the question came up with regard to if they actually became hostile and fired on our forces' ships or planes, what would our response be in these maneuvers? We notified everyone in advance that we were going to hold the maneuvers, and there was only one answer to that question. If our men are fired on, our men are going to shoot back.

"So they shot back, as you know. And there's been a lot of talk, and the press has been very concerned, because six hours went by before they awoke me at four-thirty in the morning to tell me about it. And there's a very good answer to that. Why? If our planes were shot down, yes, they'd wake me up right away; if the other fellow's were shot down, why wake me up?"

In 1980, I interviewed Nancy a few days after John Lennon of the Beatles had been shot to death by a deranged fan in New York City and asked her about her opposition to gun control.

She said that despite Lennon's death, she, like her husband, would continue to oppose gun control because she felt that, otherwise, "wrong persons" would get guns. She did not explain what she meant. Instead, she said, she favored stiffer penalties for criminals who use guns.

"I have a little gun," she volunteered. "My husband showed me how to shoot it. . . . It's a tiny little gun. Ronnie was away a lot, you know. He was out speaking a lot and I was alone in the house."

She then laughed and said she probably wouldn't need her gun now that she was going to be living in the White House with Secret Service protection. She said she never used the weapon anyway and didn't even know what kind of gun it was. "It's just a tiny little gun. I don't know anything about it."

Unrelenting turmoil marked the aftermath of the attempted assassination of Reagan in 1981, but even then, the president knew the nation's need for a few light touches and for reassurance of his fighting spirit. As he was being wheeled into the operating room, he caught sight of advisers Edwin Meese, James Baker, and Mike Deaver. "Who's minding the store?" Reagan asked. In the recovery room, Reagan had a tube in his throat and communicated via pad and pencil. "I'd like to do this scene again, starting at the hotel," he wrote.

Commenting on the respirator that was helping him breathe, he wrote, "Send me to L.A. where I can see the air I'm breathing."

* * *

The White House staff had decided against invoking the Twenty-fifth Amendment, which would have transferred power to the vice president, and about a day after the surgery, Meese, Baker, and Deaver arrived at the hospital to find Reagan propped up in bed. "I should have known I wasn't going to avoid a staff meeting," he quipped. When the three assured him that the nation's business was going on as usual despite recent events, Reagan eyed them and said, "What makes you think I'd be happy about that?"

Jim Brady had also been gravely wounded in the assassination attempt. But he also maintained a steady sense of humor. In the hospital, a doctor asked him what he did for a living. "I answer questions," said Brady. When the doctor asked for whom, Brady replied, "For anyone who asks them."

Reagan's daughter, Maureen, in her book, *First Father, First Daughter,* noted that the year she attended the Gridiron, I ran up to her at the predinner reception. "Maureen, I'm so angry—I'm playing you and they won't let me dress sexy," I complained. "They're making me do it in a pinafore and Mary Janes, and I'm really furious!"

For the performance, out I came, done up in a frilly, short dress and Mary Janes, gazed adoringly across the room, and sang (to the music of "My Heart Belongs to Daddy"):

I've led some fights for women's rights
But not as a liberal baddie
The GOP is my cup of tea
'Cause my heart belongs to Daddy
Each day I scoff at Fahrenkopf, and his '88 handicapping
My dad will choose the one who can't lose
Just as soon as he's done napping.

* * *

We now have a president who once owned a baseball team. We also had a president who had a career as an actor and who once played a famous baseball player. When members of the Baseball Hall of Fame came to the White House in late March 1981, Reagan was in his element regaling the crowd with the story of his movie portrayal of Grover Cleveland Alexander and the actual baseball players who appeared in the film:

"I remember one day when they wanted some shots of me pitching, but they had a fellow back there—well, Al Lyons, one of the ballplayers that was there, was going to catch the ball back there and then toss it back over the camera to me, and the camera was getting these close shots for use whenever they could use them. And he was on one side of the camera and my control wasn't all that it should be at one point, and I threw it on the other side of the camera. And he speared it with his left hand with no glove on. He was a left-hander and after he brought the ball to me, he said, 'Alex, I'm sorry—I had to catch your blazer bare-handed.'

"I never had more fun or enjoyed anything more than when we were making that picture. And I remember Nancy and I— we were engaged and waiting for the picture to end to get married, and she came out on a set one day and I said, 'How would you like to have a baseball autographed by all these ballplayers?' And, oh, she thought that would be great. And I started out and I looked back and there were tears in her eyes and she was standing there. And I said, 'What?' And she said, 'Can't I go get them?'"

Reagan on the basic rules of communication, told to the National Conference of Building and Construction Trades, March 1981:
"There's been a lot of talk in the last several weeks here in Washington about communication and the need to communicate.

Here is a story about some of the basic rules for communication.

"It was told to me for the first time by Danny Villanueva, who used to placekick for the Los Angeles Rams and then became a sports announcer. Danny told me that one night he was having dinner with a young ballplayer with the Los Angeles Dodgers, and the young wife was bustling about getting the dinner ready while he and the ballplayer were talking sports. And the baby started to cry, and over her shoulder the wife said to her husband, 'Change the baby.' This young ballplayer was embarrassed in front of Danny and said, 'What do you mean, change the baby? I'm a ballplayer. That's not my line of work.'

"And she turned around, put her hands on her hips, and she communicated: 'Look, buster, you lay the diaper out like a diamond, you put second base on home plate, put the baby's bottom on the pitcher's mound, hook up first and third, slide home underneath, and if it starts to rain, the game ain't called—you start all over again.'"

In September 1981, Reagan traveled to Yorktown, Virginia, and appeared at the bicentennial celebration to sign a proclamation commemorating the two hundredth anniversary of the British surrender. In his remarks, he noted that the phrase "Come let us reason together" was a favorite of President Johnson's. "It's from a verse in the Bible that begins: 'Come let us reason together,'" Reagan said. "It's probably just as well that he [Johnson] left unspoken the rest of the verse. The next line is: 'If thou refuse, thou shalt be devoured by the sword.'"

At a news conference in September 1982, ABC News correspondent Sam Donaldson tried to box Reagan in with a question about the recession:

Q: Mr. President, in talking about the continuing recession tonight, you have blamed mistakes of the past, and you've

blamed the Congress. Does any of the blame belong to you?
Reagan: Yes, because for years I was a Democrat.

I try to avoid a few things when it comes to the White House—
sporting events and pets. But UPI had Milton Richman, a legendary sportswriter. I suppose you could call him sportswriting's
equivalent to Merriman Smith—Milton always got the story
before everyone else. In 1983 my White House colleague Ira Allen
was assigned to the travel pool to cover Reagan's attendance at
the World Series opening in Baltimore. Ira recalled, "I find out that
the location of the pool will be such that we cannot do our job,
which is to keep an eye on the president. I reached Milt by
phone in the press box before we depart and ask if from his vantage point he could occasionally glance into the adjacent owner's
box to see if Reagan might be choking on a hot dog. 'Just tell me
what you want, and I'll do it,'" said Milton. Obviously, nothing
happened out of the ordinary, but if it had, there is no doubt who
would have had the advantage.

At presidential news conferences, reporters give the president a
heads-up if they plan on asking a follow-up question. Reagan
deftly dealt with the idea of two questions from one reporter in
1984, when the session was going a little long and he wanted to
hear from more reporters: "But let me—I better switch over here
for some more—and may I—a question—and I don't mean to
offend with regard to the follow-up—and I understand why you
had them, but we've been reduced to the number of questions we
get to ask when everybody has a follow-up. So ask them both at
once."

On the campaign trail in 1984, Reagan made a five-stop train tour
through the Midwest and in Ottawa, Ohio, hit his opponent Fritz
Mondale's tax plan:

"Well, now, with all this old and new Mondale, just when you're beginning to lose faith, finally you do find there is some constancy. The old Mondale increased your taxes. And the new Mondale will do it again.

"You know, in our debate, I got a little angry all those times that he distorted my record. And on one occasion, I was about to say to him very sternly, 'Mr. Mondale, you're taxing my patience.' Then I caught myself. Why should I give him another idea? That's the only tax he hasn't thought of."

From the UPI Daybook, April 18, 1984, recalled and passed on to me by David Rosso:

"The president's announced appointments for Wednesday include a morning meeting with staff and a luncheon with Catholic bishops.

"There will be a 9:30 A.M. backgrounder on the cannibal warfare treaty."

On May 9, 1984, Reagan gave the address at the Small Business Person of the Year ceremony: "You know, not too long ago, I was asked to explain the difference between a small businessman and a big businessman. And my answer was that a big businessman is what a small businessman would be if only the government would get out of the way and leave him alone."

In October 1984, Congress finished the reauthorization work on the Older Americans Act. At the signing ceremony at the White House, Reagan remarked, "I'm pleased that Congress completed action on a bill to reauthorize and improve the Older Americans Act—and it's not because I'm often reminded of what Francis Joseph Cardinal Spellman meant when he said there were three ages: youth, middle age, and 'You're looking wonderful.'"

* * *

At a state dinner in September 1981 honoring Israeli Prime Minister Menachem Begin, Reagan gave the following toast:

"Prime Minister Begin, it's a genuine pleasure to welcome you to the White House this evening—I should say, welcome you back, because the prime minister is no stranger to this room. As a matter of fact, I have a funny feeling that he may have dined here more often than I have. Be that as it may, once again, he's an honored guest. But this time Nancy and I have the privilege and we are delighted.

"I'm not sure whether you saw it or not, Mr. Prime Minister, but in the play *Fiddler on the Roof,* one of the townspeople asked the rabbi if he had a proper blessing for the czar. The rabbi answered, 'Why, of course. May God bless and keep the czar—far away from us.'

"Prime Minister Begin, as you know, the Jewish people have never been far away from sorrow and depression during their long and troubled history. And now—I don't believe your own influence on Jewish history goes as far back as the time of the czars. Now, you understand that there wouldn't be anything wrong with that. You will hear no criticism of age tolerated in this house. Lately, I've been heartened to remember that Moses was eighty when God commissioned him for public service and he lived to be one hundred twenty. And Abraham was one hundred and his wife, Sarah, ninety, when they did something truly amazing. He survived to be one hundred seventy-five. So, Mr. Prime Minister, we haven't even hit our full stride yet."

At an annual Ford's Theater benefit gala, Reagan gave due acknowledgment to the people who had worked to put together the evening's entertainment and paid a special tribute to the wives of the Democratic Speaker of the House and the Senate minority leader: "You know some people were mentioned, some credits given, you couldn't name all the people here in this theater that had a hand in making this very wonderful evening. One was mentioned, Frankie Hewitt, and she certainly deserves it. There were two ladies that I don't think any of the others would mind if I mention, who worked long and tirelessly together to make this a success: Mrs. Tip O'Neill and Mrs. Howard Baker. They worked so well together that I've got a couple of projects I'm going to suggest to their husbands. It's worth a try.

"But here in this place that is so much a part of our heritage, reminds us so much of our traditions—and, incidentally, it is not true I used to play this theater before it closed."

At a presidential news conference in July 1984, as the campaign was in full swing, the idea of Christian fellowship was mentioned when I asked Reagan the following:

Helen: Mr. President, [vice presidential candidate] Geraldine Ferraro says you're not a good Christian because—on grounds that your budget cuts have hurt the poor and the disadvantaged. Do you think you're a good Christian, and why? And I'd like to follow up.

Reagan: Well, Helen, the minute I heard she'd made that statement, I turned the other cheek.

At the Iran-contra hearings in Congress, Admiral John Poindexter was rather specific about whether he had misinformed anyone: "[It is] not fair to say that I have misinformed Congress or other cabinet officers. I haven't testified to that. I've testified that I withheld information from Congress. And with regard to the cabinet officers, I didn't withhold anything from them that they didn't want withheld from them."

Reagan was having a little trouble in 1987 with the Iran-contra situation, but he didn't duck the issue in his remarks at the annual Gridiron dinner that year:

"With the Iran thing occupying everyone's attention, I was thinking: Do you remember the flap when I said, 'We begin bombing in five minutes'? Remember when I fell asleep during my audience with the pope? Remember Bitburg? Boy, those were the good old days. I have to admit we considered making one final shipment to Iran, but no one could figure out how to get Sam Donaldson in a crate."

The president also addressed media stories that Nancy exercised some kind of undue influence on U.S. policy: "And this absurd notion about Nancy's power and influence . . ." He turned to his wife and said, "Oh, honey, I forgot to tell you. I got a call on the hot line today—it was for you.

"But, anyway, I know that this Iran thing has raised some doubts about my memory. Just yesterday, in the Oval Office, I was telling"—he turned to chief of staff Howard Baker—"uh, that man there. I said, 'Howard, my faculties are as good as they ever were.' He said, 'Yes, Mr. President, that's what concerns a lot of people.' "

Reagan also noted a speaker's remark that the president would take important papers to the White House family quarters to read during the commercial breaks while he was watching television. "That's not true," Reagan said. "I watch the commercials and read the papers during the news."

While recovering from colon surgery while the Iran-contra investigation was unfolding, Reagan remarked, "As if the independent counsel, a special review board, and two congressional committees weren't enough, there was my trip to Bethesda [Naval Hospital]. I tell you, one more probe and I've had it."

In 1988, President and Mrs. Reagan were in Moscow and decided to visit the Arbat, a pedestrian mall made up of several blocks of shops and street vendors. This spur-of-the-moment decision gave the Secret Service multiple headaches. Once the

Reagans arrived, the crowds of people realized who was there and began rushing the first couple. I was with the press pool and we began running after the president, but several KGB agents began elbowing us out of the way and knocking a few of us to the ground. Two KGB agents grabbed me and started dragging me down the street.

I started screaming, and Nancy Reagan took a few steps back, grabbed my coat, and yelled at the agents, "She's with us." They let me go, and Nancy and I walked over to where her husband was standing, and the three of us walked toward their residence.

"You owe me one, Helen," Nancy said.

Press secretary Marlin Fitzwater would say later that the White House had had another chance to get rid of me—and blew it.

President and Mrs. Reagan paid tribute in 1988 at the Kennedy Center Honors to George Burns, Myrna Loy, choreographer Alvin Ailey, violinist Alexander Schneider, and producer Roger Stevens. But Reagan reserved a special honor for Burns, ninety-two, who, the seventy-seven-year-old president said, is "the only man in America who's older than I am. The only thing I don't understand is how George Burns manages to appear with Johnny Carson so often. I'm always in bed by then."

Reagan attended his last Gridiron dinner in 1988 and had a few touching remarks for us interspersed with his masterful one-liners:

"Someday Nancy and I will be reminiscing about the Gridiron, and I'll say I remember when Carl Rowan was president, Mario Cuomo was the Democratic speaker, and you sang that song. And Nancy will say, 'Honey, that was just last night.' I'll always carry the memories of laughter in my heart, and laughter is what I will always remember about the Gridiron—that and sitting on my keister for five hours straight.

"I don't think you'll find a president who will enjoy these evenings as much as I've enjoyed them. I don't think you'll find a president who appreciates how much work the members put into this evening. You know, I've been thinking, you're really going to miss me if you have to sit through eight years of President Dukakis.

"And on that note I say to my friends in the Gridiron for the last time: Good night and thank you and God bless you all."

According to then U.S. ambassador to India Frank Wisner, sometime in 1990 an Indian told the U.S. embassy he wanted a visa in time for former President Ronald Reagan's funeral. The consular officer, somewhat taken aback, advised the applicant that Mr. Reagan was still very much alive, Wisner said.

"I'm aware of that," came the reply. "I would rather wait there than here."

Wisner did not say whether the man eventually got the U.S. visa.

GEORGE BUSH

President Bush was not one to bring big guffaws to the White House, and let's face it, Ronald Reagan—the master of the one-liner and the perfectly timed joke—was a tough act to follow.

But little did we know that he was the founder of a dynasty of disjointed communication, as his son George W. is amply demonstrating. We all caught on soon enough.

While he was quick on his feet, Bush Senior's humor more often than not was unintentional, but he was always a good sport. He used to dismiss reporters who irritated him with the line "You're history" (and I heard that one more than once) and affectionately called the photographers "photo-dogs."

While at times he did not seem to know that a sentence had a beginning, a middle, and an end, somehow he got his point across—or not. "Voodoo economics" still puzzles a few. Some of his most humorous statements cropped up when he was doing his best to be serious. During the 1988 campaign, reporters dubbed his language Bushspeak. Still, some of his phrases have become part of the vernacular: *a thousand points of light; read my lips; a kinder, gentler nation.*

"When I was in the White House," he has often said, "I believed in freedom of the press. Now I believe in freedom from the press."

Skydiving, anyone?

At a news conference on August 22, 1984, Vice President Bush singled out the next questioner: "Yes, ma'am. Right here. This lady. Do you have a question? No. She. Yes. Second row, next to the guy in the blue shirt, holding her left hand up. It's a he. Sorry about that. You got to be careful. I'm very sorry. Go ahead. Excuse me. I'm very sorry. A thousand apologies. Go ahead."

As vice president, Bush visited Twin Falls, Idaho, to deliver a speech on agricultural policy. The advance text had Bush praising all the "success" he and Ronald Reagan had enjoyed together. "For seven and a half years I've worked alongside President Reagan," said Bush. "We've had triumphs. Made some mistakes. We've had some sex—uh—setbacks . . ."

Many were sorry to see Ronald Reagan go, but I still think George Bush could have done without a remark by then–Wisconsin Governor Tommy G. Thompson, speaking on the upcoming Bush inaugural: "As the Reagan presidency ends, it is time for the Bush pregnancy to begin."

I truly don't recall the details, but a copy of this letter was making its way around the White House when George Bush was president; David Rosso kept a copy. It was addressed to:

President George Bush
White House
1600 Pennsylvania Ave.
Washington, D.C. 20500

It was dated September 17, 1992, from Van Nuys, California. It bore a U.S. Post Office stamp saying: "Return to sender. Addressee unknown."

Bush had billed himself as the "education president" and, like any president, made a number of visits to elementary and secondary schools across the country. In February 1990, during a question-and-answer session with high school students, he was asked whether his administration was getting any ideas on how to improve schools by studying education systems in other countries. "Well, I'm going to kick that one right into the end zone of the Secretary of Education," he responded. "But, yes, we have all—he travels a good deal, goes abroad. We have a lot of people in the department that does that. We're having an international—this is not as much education as dealing with the environment—a big international conference coming up. And we get it all the time—exchanges of ideas."

When it came to vice presidents, though, Bush's veep, Dan Quayle, was no slouch in the "What did he say?" department. On a visit to Hawaii in 1989, he pointed out, "Hawaii has always been a very pivotal role in the Pacific. It *is* in the Pacific. It is a part of the United States that is an island that is right here."

And who could ever forget his galvanizing speech at an affair honoring the United Negro College Fund, which has for years had the slogan "A mind is a terrible thing to waste."

"What a waste it is to lose one's mind," Quayle said, "or not to have a mind. How true that is."

A reporter asked Quayle, then the vice presidential candidate, his opinion of the Holocaust. He responded:

"[The Holocaust] was an obscene period in our nation's history . . . this century's history. We all lived in this century. I didn't live in this century."

Ann Richards, then the Democratic governor of Texas, brought the house down at the Democratic National Convention in 1988 when she noted that then–Vice President Bush was "born with a silver foot in his mouth." She had a point, among others. Bush also made the following gaffes during the campaign:

"I'm going to be coming out here with my own drug problem."

"I hope I stand for antibigotry, anti-Semitism, antiracism. This is what drives me."

"I will make sure that everyone who has a job wants a job."

From 1988, passed along by UPI reporter Mark Ridolfi: slapped on the bumper of his car parked in the garage of the *Indianapolis News:* "H.E.A.D. (Hoosiers Embarrassed About Dan)."

Quayle's grandfather owned the paper.

In 1989, Bush was getting a little annoyed at the tone of stories being written about him, implying he was boring. But at the 1989 White House Correspondents Association dinner, he said he was getting the hint "even though it makes me mad when Helen Thomas ends a news conference with 'Thank you, Barbara's husband.' "

I will say that when it came to Gridiron speeches, President Bush was a good sport. In his remarks in March 1990, he complimented the group on its rousing finale and reminded us of the previous year's dinner when Mrs. Bush had sported a strawberry-blond wig:

"That closer a few moments ago was the most rousing thing I've seen in over a dozen Gridirons," he said. "But I also remember an inspired moment Barbara and I had, after last year's dinner. Standing on a windy street corner, she in a trench coat with the collar turned up, her long, flowing red hair blowing in the wind, and both of us too proud to run after it."

Nodding to Gridiron president David Broder of the *Washington Post,* Bush congratulated him on his office: "It's good to have an intellectual in charge at last. It took vision to predict my race would be over after Iowa. It took depth to say [Michael] Dukakis would get the Southern vote. . . . It takes clairvoyance to work for a paper that, three days before the election, predicts Daniel Ortega by thirty points. Speech in the dark? Hell, Broder writes whole columns in the dark."

Bush went on to note the relationship between the press corps and his able spokesman, Marlin Fitzwater: "To all here, let me express my appreciation for your cooperation with our press secretary. But he's come a long way from last year, when he went into a clothing store. Marlin said, 'I'd like to see a bathing suit in my size.' And the clerk said, 'So would I.'"

Bush closed with a warm thought—but a pointed jab—at the sport the press had taken with his grammatical lapses: "We may witness the world's upheavals through eyes blurred with tears, or eyes bright with wonder. But we can know that, because of this idea called America, the world will never be the same again. And thanks to my best efforts—and your indelicacy in pointing out my best efforts—the English language may never be the same again, either."

In 1989 the pilots of Eastern Airlines went on strike. President Bush was being urged to take a role in the negotiations and said, "I still feel that the best answer is a head-on-head, man-to-man negotiation between the union and the airline."

In September 1965, Lyndon Johnson had signed the National Foundation of the Arts and Humanities Act. In September 1989, George and Barbara Bush attended a gala event commemorating that legislation, which had created the American Film Institute. The first couple sat with Lynda Johnson Robb and her husband, Democratic Senator Chuck Robb of Virginia. One of the evening's entertainments featured talk show host Phil Donahue introducing various audience members, who each took a turn at the microphone and recited famous lines from films. NBC

President Brandon Tartikoff chose the Howard Beale line from the movie *Network*—"I'm mad as hell and I'm not going to take it anymore"—and then–Defense Secretary Dick Cheney intoned, "May the Force be with you," from *Star Wars*.

They were followed by the duo of critics Roger Ebert and Gene Siskel, who did a series of "instant reviews" on the one-liners. Siskel wrapped up their set by commenting on Bush's predecessor: "Can you believe it? Eight years with a movie actor in the White House and we never got invited?"

During the 1992 New Hampshire primary, Bush noted in a speech, "Remember Lincoln, going to his knees in times of trial in the Civil War and all that stuff. You can't be. And we are blessed. So don't feel sorry for—don't cry for me, Argentina." (To this day, some members of the press corps are trying to figure that one out.)

I've always given White House pets a wide berth and the Bush dogs were no exception. However, one day—the particulars escape me but it has been captured on video—Bush was returning to the White House and the limousine drove up to the front entrance. I was standing behind the rope line with the rest of the press corps, and one of the dogs, Millie or Ranger, came bounding out and headed straight for me. A small shriek can be heard off-camera, and Bush turns around to see what all the commotion is about.

"What happened?" he asks, and someone out of camera range tells him. Bush turns back to head into the White House and can be heard muttering, "Sic 'errrrr . . ."

During a visit to the Golan Heights, a Jordanian army captain asked Bush if he had any questions. Yes, he said. "How dead is the Dead Sea?"

*   *   *

In the garbled syntax that Bush was prone to, he gave an interview to Joan Lunden on *Good Morning America* in October 1992, shortly before the election:

Lunden: All right, President Bush, thank you very much for joining us this morning, talking about the issue of crime. And President Bush will be back with us again on Friday. We'll talk about the crisis in health care. Thank you.

Bush: It's a crime we're not having debates.

Lunden: All right. Well . . .

Bush: Get it?

Lunden: Those are yet to be seen.

Bush: Okay.

In their interview, Lunden touched on the increase in homelessness and the rise in welfare statistics:

Lunden: A lot of people are troubled by the fact there has been a significant increase in the number of families on the welfare rolls since you took office—just about a twenty-eight percent increase, about another million families on the rolls. How do you explain those numbers?

Bush: Well, we're going through very tough economic times. We've had a slow growth period, anemic growth, and when that happens . . . but then when you have that, why, more people are on welfare.

At a news conference in 1992, I began questioning Bush with the following:

HT: Mr. President, are you going to go for a middle-income tax cut and are you going to cut the Pentagon budget by $80 billion and are you going to break the budget agreement—and I'd like a follow-up . . ."

Bush: Helen, you have six days to wait for the answers to all those questions.

* * *

Sometimes Bush's strange vocabulary made its way to the White House staff. On October 20, 1992, after the debate with Bill Clinton, campaign press aide Torie Clark commented, "He [Bush] showed tonight he is a man who looks into the abyss, sucks it up, and comes out punching."

Herb Caen's column: "You'll have to take Lou Torres's word for it. At the Prime Rib Inn in Palo Alto, he overheard this kid, about ten, tell his mother, 'I'm so sore at Eddie, I'm gonna kick his ass.' Mom: 'Don't talk like that.' Kid: 'George Bush does.' Mom: 'Then I don't want you to play with him.' "

As the onetime head of the CIA, George Bush obviously learned how to keep a secret. But his plans for a surprise birthday party for his wife, Barbara, were nearly compromised through an unlikely leak.

In June 2000, Bush planned a Saturday-night party for his wife, who would turn seventy-five two days earlier, at the family's home in Kennebunkport, Maine. All five of their children and fourteen grandchildren would attend.

However, former Senator Alan Simpson of Wyoming almost deep-sixed the secret when he called to apologize for being unable to attend.

Mrs. Bush knew her family was attending but was surprised to find 185 guests, including former Joint Chiefs Chairman Colin Powell, the Saudi Ambassador Prince Bandar Bin Sultan, and a number of friends from Houston. But later she said it was probably just as well that someone had let the details slip. "It was such a big, wonderful party, I might have died," she said.

In August 2000, George and Barbara Bush made a surprise visit to the Florida delegation at the Republican National Convention in Philadelphia. The former president made his feelings clear about the media treatment of his son George, who was about to accept the nomination for president. He almost called the nominee his "boy" but stopped short, recalling the negative fallout after he had made a similar remark in New Hampshire.

"The national press went ballistic," Bush told the delegates as his wife, Barbara, his son Jeb, the governor of Florida, and Jeb's family stood behind him. It was "the nastiest, meanest kind of reporting I've seen. So I've got to be very, very careful."

However, all bets were off when it came to Mrs. Bush. "We unleash Barbara from time to time," he said. "Only forty-eight hours to go and no land mines have really exploded, although this morning on ABC's *Good Morning America* she went semiballistic."

Barbara used her remarks to apologize for her husband: "I don't like to criticize, but several years ago he joined Press Bashers Anonymous. And he had a little slippage today. I promise you he's going back on the wagon right now."

On the show, the two were asked what it was like to be the parents of the Republican nominee for president rather than hoping to occupy the White House themselves as they had successfully done in 1988 before losing in 1992. Barbara said, "I was much nicer in 1992 and 1988."

"Barbara probably went further today than she should have," said her husband.

During a state visit to Japan, television viewers everywhere were shocked to see President Bush, who was suffering from a bad case of the flu, slump in his chair and throw up all over the Japanese prime minister. A few years later, Bush invited the dignitary to the opening of the Bush Presidential Library in Texas and included a note: "Dinner's on me."

BILL CLINTON

He ran for so many class and club offices that his high school principal had to bar him from campaigning for any more. As the nation's first postwar baby-boom-generation president, he brought a new kind of attitude to the White House, for better or for worse.

He had them rolling in the aisles at the annual Gridiron and White House Correspondents Association dinners. He had the help of writer Mark Katz and others, and occasionally his young, irreverent staffers threw in their nickel's worth.

He was sharp, but Kennedy and Reagan had a better sense of when to dig in with a one-liner. He learned, though, and he showed up—courageously, I thought—at the dinners when he knew he was going to be lampooned unmercifully at the time of revelations about the Monica Lewinsky affair and of the impeachment proceedings.

Somehow, he was able to take it and give it back. When radio personality Don Imus took crude aim at him at a Radio-Television Correspondents dinner, Clinton didn't flinch.

A tough skin, an inner confidence, and a faith that "this too shall pass" somehow sustained him and his sense of humor. And when he turned self-deprecating, audiences loved it.

His last appearance at the White House Correspondents Association dinner in April 2000 was, to many, the gold standard of such appearances. His "The Final Days" video, depicting him as a powerless lame duck roaming the empty halls of the White

House, looking for something to do, chasing after his Senate-campaigning wife with her lunch bag, washing the presidential limousine, clipping hedges, answering telephones, and then hitting on the right combination of how to spend his last days—a golf ball ticking the hood of Representative Dan Burton's car among others—garnered no less than a standing ovation and his own Oscar. It was a worthy performance.

On his first presidential campaign, Clinton responded to Vice President Dan Quayle's remark that he would be a "pit bull" in helping the Republicans retain the White House: "That's got every fire hydrant in America worried."

Coping with laryngitis, Clinton said, "My doctor ordered me to shut up, which will make every American happy."

Clinton was introduced at a debate as the smartest of the candidates seeking the Democratic nomination. "Isn't that like calling Moe the most intelligent of the Three Stooges?" he asked.

Ironies never cease at the White House. When Clinton was elected to his first term in 1992, the *Washington Post* ran a story that former Joint Chiefs Chairman Colin Powell would be named Secretary of State.

In December, I was invited to a Christmas party at Sam Donaldson's home and spotted Powell among the guests. In my usual shy way, I marched up to him and said, "General, are you going to be the next Secretary of State?"

Powell looked at me, then turned to another guest and said, "Isn't there some war we can send her to?"

Well, now he is Secretary of State in George W. Bush's cabinet, and after his confirmation I got a note from him: "I'm still looking for that war."

Who could resist? I wrote back, "Hell no, I won't go."

* * *

Much has been written about the chaos in the White House when President Clinton took office in 1993. This was reflected in the way the press secretary, Dee Dee Myers, and communications director, George Stephanopoulos, were treating the White House press corps. David Rosso remembered a letter I sent to UPI's Washington bureau chief Frank Csongos trying to make the point that the Clinton White House, to put it charitably, was going through terrible growing pains:

"Dear Frank: I think a letter of complaint should be written to press secretary Dee Dee Myers, who called our office at 12:30 A.M. saying an announcement was forthcoming by fax. She did not disclose the subject and the fax never arrived. At around 2:30 A.M. the desk scrambled and received from audio the announcement which audio had obtained from Fox Television. Furthermore, when the desk called the White House there was no press duty officer, and the switchboard would not put us through to Dee Dee. This is a helluva way to run a railroad and has frightening prospects for the future if they continue to do business that way. Thomas-WHU."

What was the fax all about? Here's the story:

Bc-baird-fax 1–22
Baird withdrawal announced by fax
WASHINGTON (UPI)—President Clinton Friday announced by fax to wire services and the television networks the fact that he had accepted Zoe Baird's request to withdraw her nomination as attorney general.

Then there was this story I filed on February 3, 1993:

Bc-clinton-watch
Will he or won't he?
WASHINGTON (UPI)—President Clinton left the Clinton watchers in the cold again Wednesday.

The press pool gathered outside the White House before dawn, ready to report on whether the chief executive went for his predawn jog through the streets of the nation's capital.

They sat and waited. Inside a van. For two hours.

They saw the dawn of a new day, but not The Man.

They saw Socks, the first cat, being led around the White House grounds on a long leash.

They saw Clinton's daughter, Chelsea, dressed in blue jeans, leave the White House and get into a black car with her female Secret Service agent to go to school.

But they did not see the president of the United States run.

Perhaps it was Wednesday morning's below-freezing temperatures.

On Tuesday, when Clinton prepared to hit the road running, the temperature in downtown Washington was fourteen degrees with a windchill index of about eleven degrees below zero.

Clinton opted to skip his morning jog Tuesday and, instead, walked from the White House to the gym in the Executive Office Building next door to work out.

I was president of the Gridiron Club when Clinton attended his first dinner in March 1993. Senator Bob Dole of Kansas made much of the dress I'd chosen that night, noting that it came from "the J. Edgar Hoover collection."

At that dinner, we got an inkling of what Clinton's humor would be like for the next eight years (give or take a few, with a scandal here and there).

"What a thrill it is to be at my first Gridlock dinner," he told us. "Preeminent among you is my great dinner companion, the first lady of White House journalism, Helen Thomas. . . . She hurt my feelings when she said she didn't want to see me in my bathrobe. . . . I've always been curious about your body. As dean of the White House press corps, she's been keeping presidents honest for thirty years. She's spent more time in the

White House than anybody here tonight. Still, it hurt my feelings when she demanded a security deposit when we moved in. Helen's been in Washington so long, she remembers when the Electoral College was a high school."

Here we go again with those souvenir pens: In May 1993, Clinton's troubles with Congress were hitting their stride, and one Republican lawmaker had been more than peeved for almost four months. Republican Representative Marge Roukema of New Jersey, who had supported the Family and Medical Leave Act, was a little annoyed she had never got a commemorative pen from the bill signing in February. "I was really stunned that they weren't organized at the White House for what is a rather pro forma procedure with landmark legislation," she said. Roukema had gone as far as to formally request her souvenir, but without success. "How many contortions does a member of Congress—who's put in blood, sweat, and tears and even gone against her [party]— have to go through?" she said. "One can understand that initially it was a lack of experience, but . . . there's no excuse for not understanding the significance."

It turned out that Clinton had given away all the pens he used at the ceremony. Roukema eventually received her own personally signed copy of the bill.

Les Aspin, a former Indiana congressman and Clinton's first Defense Secretary, had us all wondering when he was discussing the Pentagon budget before Congress early in the administration:

"It's not just a defense budget by subtraction. A lot of things will be cut, but other things will be increased. There will be a series of increases and decreases. The net result of the increases and decreases will be a net cut, but it certainly is not going to be as big as the gross cut from adding up the cuts."

* * *

April 13, 1993, press briefing with Dee Dee Myers:

Myers: Good morning. The only two events on the president's schedule today are the 250th anniversary of the birth of Thomas Jefferson at noon at the Jefferson Memorial, which is open to the press. And at 8:30 P.M. he will participate in a satellite town meeting with Chamber of Commerce around the country at the Chamber of Commerce Building. And that will be thirty minutes.

Q: What's his speech? Will it be strictly devoted to the Declaration of Independence and so forth?

Myers: He'll talk about Jefferson but I think he will tie it to current events.

Q: Like the [economic] stimulus package?

Q: Jefferson would have passed the stimulus package?

Q: Jefferson would have voted for stimulus, is that it?

Myers: All things are connected in our world. Someone pointed out yesterday the Louisiana Purchase was the largest stimulus package in the history of the country. I don't think that's in the speech, though.

At his first White House Correspondents Association dinner in May 1993, Clinton responded to all the criticism and attacks on the early days of his term. "I'm not doing so bad," he said. "At this point in his administration, William Henry Harrison had been dead sixty-eight days!" Clinton also made much of the "report card" the press was prone to use on him and recalled how when he was in law school, his mother used to keep "my grades posted on her refrigerator . . . of course, Hillary's were higher."

On June 2, 1993, Canadian Prime Minister Brian Mulroney appeared on the *MacNeil/Lehrer Newshour* and was asked about his comment that "it's nonsense to suggest that Clinton's presidency 'is broken.'" His response: "Well, I referred to what can only be described as a quaint American custom, where you elect a president for four years and then you decide after one hundred days whether he's dead or alive. This is pretty silly stuff. Nobody can resolve the problems that confront a great nation in one hundred days, and I understand the tradition from Roosevelt and so on, and everybody appears to be measured by this standard, but it's not a helpful thing to do.

"The problems of the United States, and the problems of Canada, the U.K., and others, are problems so complex and intractable that they require mature judgment and strong leadership over an extended period of time. Give the guy a break. He just started. Let him see what he can do over a period of time, and the beauty of a democracy is you throw us in or you throw us out after a period of time. That's four years, or five years, depending on the British parliamentary system, not one hundred days. I think it's kind of unhelpful to anyone, including to the United States, to pass these kinds of definitive and quite vitriolic judgments about a president who has just received the confidence of the American people and say after ninety days or one hundred days, 'By the way, you're through. Let's turn our attention to somebody else.'"

David Rosso filed this Clinton quote to UPI bureaus on June 12, 1993, under the heading "How not to answer the question that isn't the question you wanted to answer." It was from Clinton's Earth Summit news conference in Washington and had something to do with reducing carbon dioxide emissions in the United States and what the level would be at the end of his administration.

"Well," said Clinton, "that's not the right way to ask the question. The question I can answer is 'Would I have signed a treaty in 1992 which would have said by the year 2000, which is the end of the second term, that we would get back to 1990 levels of emission?' The answer to that is, yes, I would have been glad to sign that treaty, and I believe that would have created jobs in America and not cost jobs in America."

On August 4, 1993, one of the stranger news briefings with White House aide Mark Gearan took place. We couldn't quite get a handle on the president's schedule for the next week after Gearan said, "This weekend he'll be here, most likely."

Q: And he travels Monday, and then he's here Tuesday and Wednesday and then he goes out Thursday?

Gearan: Right.

Q: Doesn't he go out Wednesday? He doesn't go out Wednesday?

Gearan: Possibly out—this is just for guidance purposes. Possibly out Wednesday night.

Q: For Denver?

Q: In other words, could we leave early?

Gearan: You can all leave anytime you want. The bus leaves at 2 P.M., be under it.

He closed the session saying, "I've been informed that today is Helen Thomas's birthday. And in our continuing effort to embarrass members of the press, we invite you to join with Dee Dee Myers in singing 'Happy Birthday' to—"

Helen: Please don't.

Gearan: For those of you in the back of the room, Helen said—

At which point people started shouting "Speech!" and Gearan further noted, "The gift is wrapped in UPI paper," and told me to open it.

"I don't dare," I said, which prompted more calls of "We want you to open it! We dare you to open it!"

Gearan: Helen, could you say "thank you" so we can get out of here?

"Thank you."

* * *

Midway through Clinton's first term, I made an appearance on *Late Show with David Letterman.* He asked me, "So, who do you like as a candidate in the next election?"

"Do I have to like *any* of them?" I replied.

Vice President and Mrs. Gore threw some unforgettable children's Halloween parties at their residence, and one was particularly unforgettable for me. I was there with my nieces Judy Jenkins and Terri DeLeon and their children. Al Gore had dressed up as Frankenstein's monster, complete with green makeup and a bolt in his neck, and Tipper was decked out as the bride of Frankenstein.

White House aide Mark Gearan came in and told me that "someone had shot up the White House."

"Oh, my God," I said. "Is this some kind of joke?"

I called the copy desk and was told that, yes, a man had fired a semiautomatic rifle through the White House gates and hit a few windows in the pressroom, but the Secret Service and police had subdued him.

A few days later I ran into Gearan and we started talking about the incident. I told him about the terror I'd felt, wondering whether the president had been shot.

"You know," said Gearan, "all I could think about was Al Gore being sworn in as president dressed up like Frankenstein."

There have been all kinds of White House pets. The Clintons' cat, Socks, was probably one of the few I got along with because I hardly ever saw him, and when I did, he was on a leash. Socks was a popular figure, though, and even had about five thousand people who had enrolled in the fan club run by Jay Jacob Wind of Arlington, Virginia, who also marketed all kinds of Socks memorabilia. Wind did get to meet the first feline, who appeared with

Hillary Rodham Clinton during the holiday season at Children's Hospital in Washington. Wind got to hold Socks briefly before the cat got restless.

"I've waited so long for this moment. I've done so much for you," Wind said he told Socks, who, he noted later, "didn't seem to pay any attention."

Press briefing with Dee Dee Myers, October 22, 1993:

Helen: Do you know the general topic for tomorrow's radio address?

Myers: Tomorrow's radio address will be on crime.

Helen: Pro or con?

Myers: The president's weighing his options on that.

In June 1994, the Clintons hosted a White House dinner, and guest Whoopi Goldberg was more interested in watching basketball than the scheduled entertainment.

Vice President Gore told her, "I think I can take care of that," and got her a TV set from the car. During the postdinner recital, Goldberg gazed at the small screen, rooting for the New York Knicks over the Houston Rockets.

A few minutes later, Clinton joined her for a bit. Someone asked Clinton which team he was rooting for.

"I've made enough decisions for one day!" he said.

At her last briefing in December 1994, press secretary Dee Dee Myers delivered her version of a "Top 10 List" so popular on *Late Show with David Letterman,* outlining what she would not miss about the job:

10. Helen Thomas.
9. Air Force One food.
8. Twenty-four-hour-a-day paging, late-night phone calls, and those early-morning baggage calls.

7. The soft, quiet, reflective questioning of Sarah McClendon.
6. The fact that my busy social calendar has made it often difficult to get back to the president and to all of you—busy returning those phone calls.
5. Bureau chiefs, editors, and especially headline writers.
4. The ongoing and breathtaking attention span of certain network correspondents, who can simultaneously question and do crossword puzzles.
3. That daily crush to make it to my briefing on time so as not to miss the opening.
2. Did I mention Helen Thomas?
   Finally, the number one thing that I will not miss: All of this . . . That's only half-true.

In 1995, Clinton traveled to New York for the opening of the U.N. General Assembly and had arranged for a private dinner with several heads of state. The "pool report"—compiled by a designated White House reporter traveling with the president and then disseminated to other media outlets—had a certain "woof" quality. National Security Council chief Tony Lake was briefing reporters on those who were not invited to the dinner and was asked how the White House justified keeping some off the guest list.

"Well, it's kind of like 'the dog ate the invitations,' you know?" said Lake.

"Dog invitations?" asked someone, and Lake then made a barking sound.

The pool report filed later stated, "About 140 chiefs of missions and heads of state are invited. The official said that only the 'dog nations' were not invited to the president's reception."

On August 4, 1995, the White House staff threw me a surprise party on my seventy-fifth birthday. I had been in the Oval Office interviewing Clinton—my "gift" was fifteen minutes one-on-one, but Vice President Gore broke up the session a little beforehand, and the two of them escorted me back to the pressroom.

I'd left my tape recorder on the president's desk, but he had nimbly picked it up on the way out. He turned it on and shoved it in my face:

"Miss Thomas," he said, "all these years, listening to all these presidents, listening to all the double-talk, all the confusion, catching people in lies, the deceit . . . how have you stood it for so long?"

"My sentiments, exactly," I replied.

Daily briefing with press secretary Mike McCurry, January 2, 1996 (the government had been shut down a second time as Clinton vetoed the budget from Congress):

McCurry: Happy New Year to all of you, and here is the first White House briefing of 1996. Let's make it a short one.

Helen: Let's make it real.

McCurry: Make it real. Okay, let's make it real, Helen. Go.

Helen: Okay. How long is the president going to tolerate this club over his head and over the nation in terms of shutting down the government?

McCurry: Well, if the president could take that club and throw it into the fireplace and burn it and get this government open again, he would do so on his own. But we have a constitutional system here that has branches of government, and the other branch of government has not sent to the president a sufficient measure to open the government.

A daily briefing with Mike McCurry, February 13, 1996:

McCurry: What would you all like to talk about today?

Q: What is the message you take out of Iowa?

McCurry: That the Democratic Party is united and enthusiastic behind our president. The Iowa caucuses were, for the president, very gratifying. I'm sure you all saw the *Des Moines Register* headline, "Clinton Visit Inspires Democrats to Turn Out." Over fifty thousand did, even though the president, of course, was unopposed. The president did pretty well squeak by, got 99.8 percent of the vote and all of the delegates. He was very encouraged by—

HT: Just like in the Soviet Union.

At the 1997 Gridiron, most of the talk was about Al Gore and what had to be one of the funniest speeches he ever gave, and of President Clinton, who was recovering from a fall he took at golfer Greg Norman's house in Florida. Clinton, via video from Bethesda Naval Hospital, spoke of the advantages of cloning himself and quipped, "I'm in no condition to do a stand-up routine. I feel my pain."

Gore, who was pinch-hitting for Clinton, poked fun at himself and the latest rash of bad publicity. He said that when he asked the president if he was looking forward to the Gridiron dinner, Clinton replied he'd rather fall down a flight of stairs. Gore reported that Clinton required only local anesthesia for his knee surgery, not the general anesthesia Gore had received before his most recent news conference, in which he had defended his fund-raising calls yet vowed to call no more. (Gore also was taking heat for a visit to a Buddhist monastery where he made an alleged pitch for campaign funds.)

The biggest laugh came when he said the Democrats had upped their standards and issued a challenge to congressional Republicans: "And so I say to you Senator Lott: up yours." (Majority Leader Trent Lott of Mississippi, by the way, was not there.)

Comedian and author Al Franken, who was a guest, told a member that at one point during the evening the Secret Service had pulled him away from his table to ask if he thought the "up yours" joke would succeed. He had said he thought it was humorous, but he'd provided Gore a backup remark just in case it bombed, something to the effect of "Well, the Zen master thought it was funny."

In the hit number of the 1997 Gridiron, a limited member portrayed Hillary Rodham Clinton, who had been getting some press about her "conversations" with Eleanor Roosevelt. Randall Brooks, as Eva Peron, sang:

> Don't cry for me, Mrs. Roosevelt,
> Don't worry about indictment.
> My former law firm, Rose is the name,
> By any other
> Would smell the same.

To the strains of "The Macarena," journalists dressed as Buddhist monks sang:

> Welcome, Mr. Gore, to our money-raising temple.
> You'll find that our ethics are very, very simple.
> Furthermore we're exempt from a Kenneth Starr
>   subpoena—
> Hey, macarena!

Press secretary Mike McCurry avoided all questions pertaining to Monica Lewinsky even when the press corps persisted in asking them.

One day in January 1998, yet another Monica question came up and he responded, "I'll refer you to my transcript yesterday, which referred to my transcript the day before."

By March 1998, the Monica Lewinsky situation was heating up precipitously and Clinton was being battered from all sides. Independent Counsel Kenneth Starr was expanding his investigation to include the Lewinsky allegations, and on January 17, Clinton had been deposed in the Paula Jones lawsuit.

At that year's Gridiron, he opened his remarks with "So, how was *your* week? For one hundred thirteen years, the Gridiron Club has honored its one defining rule: 'Gridiron humor singes but never burns.' And I've got the singe marks to prove it. But tonight, given Washington's current political climate, I'd like to request that the people in this room honor a second rule, and that is: kindly withhold your subpoenas until all the jokes have been told.

"This is an unusual time in Washington. Our version of 'March Madness.' So my preparation for this Gridiron speech was a little different than in years past. In fact, I wasn't even sure if I was going to come tonight. My political team told me I had to. My legal team advised me not to. My national security team suggested I hold a Gridiron town meeting. So I went to my trusted press secretary, Mike McCurry, for his advice. And here's the speech he helped me write:

" 'Good evening, ladies and gentlemen of the Gridiron. I have nothing further for you on that. Thank you and good night, and, *no*, Helen, I will not parse "good evening" for you.' "

Still, Clinton made the most of legalese humor by describing some material the counsel's office had sent over that it deemed funny: "A lawyer and his client walk into a bar. The client turns to his lawyer and says—no, wait. That's privileged. And here's my favorite: 'Knock, knock.' 'Don't answer that!' Lawyers whose names I can mention: Daniel Webster, Clarence Darrow, Ally McBeal. Independent prosecutors whose names I can mention: Lawrence Walsh. People named Starr I can mention: Brenda, Bart, Ringo. The lawyers also told me that this year, I can tell as many Lincoln Bedroom jokes as I want and I just did. What a difference a year makes. Last year I threw myself down a flight of stairs to avoid coming to the Gridiron. This year, it's worse. I've come to the Gridiron to avoid going to the movies."

* * *

December 1998: The country is in the throes of the impeachment proceedings against President Clinton; the House of Representatives began its debate on December 18, but aides depicted Clinton as too busy with other matters to pay attention. At a news briefing, press aide Joe Lockhart said Clinton had done "very little" in the last day to stave off his impeachment, which became nearly a mathematical certainty, as every Republican pledged to vote against him. Lockhart said he had just dropped by to see the president and described his mood as very good, citing a good night's sleep, the safe return of U.S. pilots from their raids on Iraq, and the holiday season.

I had only one question: "Is he out of his mind?"

By March 1999 the Comeback Kid had come back all over again. The impeachment trial was over, and to the assembled Gridiron guests, Clinton noted, "On the way over here, my press secretary, Joe Lockhart, reminded me of his pledge that the White House would be a gloat-free zone. Hey, Joe, this is not the White House."

Clinton did note, though, "I won't kid you. This was an awful year. It was a year I wouldn't wish on my worst enemy. No, I take that back. In these past thirteen months, I've learned valuable political lessons. Important personal lessons. And more than I ever cared to know about the presidency of Andrew Johnson. But that year is behind us. Yesterday I even saw fit to hold a press conference. And you know, it wasn't so bad. I enjoyed it so much, I just scheduled another for next year."

On that long-awaited news conference, Joe Lockhart had joked with reporters that Clinton had planned it "because he's been watching some of my daily briefings and he sees how much trouble you give me on a daily basis, and he said, 'I really ought to hold a news conference.'"

Lockhart also said the plan was to hold a news conference a month, much to the shock of the assembled, and then quickly rebounded, "That may be a little ambitious, but we can certainly try."

April 2, 1999, the White House Correspondents Association dinner. After a year in which he had endured an impeachment trial in the Senate and seen his life's most intimate moments spelled out to the public, it would seem the last place President Clinton would want to be would be in a large room filled with reporters. But he showed up late enough to miss the presentation of an award to *Newsweek* magazine writer Michael Isikoff, who had dedicated the last year to unearthing the Monica Lewinsky scandal. Clinton managed to joke about the press, telling the crowd of two thousand that "veteran reporter Helen Thomas was upset at a proposal to move the briefing room because she remembered the last time it moved—when the capital changed from Philadelphia to Washington."

"I like the job," he said to me in an interview in 1999. "The bad days are part of it. I didn't run to have a pleasant time, I ran to have the chance to change the country, and if the bad days come with it—that's part of life and it's humbling and educational. It keeps you in your place."

By July 1999 the president seemed positively relaxed. In the East Room, one of the reporters complained it was difficult to see him because of the bright arc lights behind his head. "I have waited a long time for a halo," joked Clinton, and the room broke up with laughter.

October 4, 1999: A year ago, when Joe Lockhart replaced Mike McCurry as White House press secretary, a lot of reporters hoped he would emulate his predecessor, considered the gold standard of modern press secretaries. But he's been winning ovations for doing things his way. He also benefited from the waning scandal coverage and perhaps from his boss's mellowing out from that famous temper of his. "It's the best job I ever had and I can't wait until it's over," he said.

Clinton press conference, February 16, 2000:

Helen: Mr. President, you don't seem to have any good news on the Northern Ireland and Middle Eastern front, so I thought I'd ask you a home-front question. How do you like being targeted in the Republican presidential campaign? Texas Governor—I have to quote this—Texas Governor Bush told Senator McCain, "Whatever you do, don't equate my integrity and trustworthiness with Bill Clinton. That's about as low as you can get in the Republican primary." And McCain said he resented being called "Clinton" or "Clinton-like" and a few other things. What do you say?

Clinton: Well, I have a couple of observations. One is, you know they're playing to the electorate, most of whom did not vote for me. And secondly, I have a lot of sympathy with Governor Bush and Senator McCain. I mean, it's hard for them to figure out what to run on. They can't run against the longest economic expansion in history; or the lowest crime rate in thirty years; or the lowest welfare rolls in thirty years; or the progress America has made in promoting peace around the world; or that fact that our party overrode theirs and passed the family leave, and it's benefited 20 million people and it hasn't hurt the economy. So they've got a tough job, and I have a lot of sympathy for them. And I don't want to complicate their problems by saying any more about them.

Q: You say you're not running this year, but you are casting a shadow over the debate on the campaign trail.

Clinton: I'd like to think I'm casting a little sunshine over it.

I keep trying to build these fellows up, you know, I'm being nice and generous and all that.

Q: All of the candidates are running against your behavior and your conduct—not just the Republicans, as Helen mentioned, but all of the candidates.

Clinton: Well, if I were running, I'd do that.

First daughter Chelsea Clinton accompanied her father on a trip to South Asia in early 2000. Caught in a parental moment, Clinton said he was thrilled Chelsea had come along with him. "You know, when your child grows up—I think any parent with a grown child can identify with this—you're always sort of pleasantly surprised when they still want to hang around with you a little," Clinton said at a press conference. My former UPI White House colleague Ken Bazinet, now with the New York *Daily News,* had first caught wind the previous December that Chelsea would be filling in for her New York Senate candidate mom. He reported that Clinton added, "Anytime I can be with her, I want to be with her." Chelsea, that is.

When good cars go bad and how press secretaries deal with it:

In April 2000, Clinton traveled to Nevada and later played a round of golf. Thanks to a spare limo, Clinton made his tee time. The motorcade carrying the first duffer was forced to halt briefly when his limousine started billowing smoke on Interstate 15 along Las Vegas's fabled Strip. Clinton hopped into the extra limousine that accompanies him in the motorcade and was on the road again within minutes.

"It went a lot smoother than most of my breakdowns go," said White House spokesman Jake Siewert.

The stories of Clinton's congenital inability to get anywhere on time are legion. However, even he pushed the envelope when he kept his mother-in-law, Dorothy Rodham, cooling her heels in the presidential helicopter, Marine One, for ninety minutes before they headed to the Clintons' new home in New York.

But Mrs. Rodham might have cut him some slack this time. Clinton got caught up in a conversation with former President Jimmy Carter, who was paying a visit to his onetime home.

In April 2000, the White House incurred the wrath of the press corps when actor Leonardo DiCaprio, star of the blockbuster movie *Titanic,* was granted an interview with Clinton for an Earth Day special on ABC.

Was the sit-down interview a spur-of-the-moment thing—as the network insisted—or did it result from lengthy negotiations, as the White House contended? And just what role was DiCaprio performing for ABC News when he interviewed Clinton—journalist or viewer-drawing celeb?

ABC had insisted that DiCaprio's assigned role was to take a walking tour with Clinton to spotlight environmental changes made to the White House. Then at the last minute, a spokeswoman noted that the walk-through was canceled for an impromptu sit-down interview.

ABC staffers were outraged that the network had given the plum assignment to a movie actor. ABC News chief David Westin sent a staff memo saying "no one is that stupid" as to send DiCaprio to conduct a presidential interview for ABC News. But DiCaprio spokesman Ken Sunshine said the actor arrived at the White House expecting to interview Clinton "walking or sitting" and came prepared with cards bearing questions.

And when asked at a news briefing to characterize the session, Joe Lockhart expressed his certainty that "it was an interview. If there is another term . . . for that, I'm not aware of it."

At the Radio-Television Correspondents annual dinner after all of the "Leo imbroglio," President Clinton rose to speak and the theme song for *Titanic* boomed out over the sound system.

He joked that ABC had been waffling. The network didn't know if DiCaprio had done an "interview, a walk-through, or a drive-by," he quipped.

"Don't you newspeople ever learn?" Clinton asked the audience. "It isn't the mistake that kills you. It's the cover-up."

In his last appearance at the White House Correspondents Association dinner in late April 2000, President Clinton was given an A for attending all eight dinners during his administration. Not a bad feat, considering the slings and arrows that punctuated them. And he made the most of reflecting on those eight turbulent years in his speech, saying, "The record on that count is clear: in good days and bad, in times of great confidence or great controversy, I have actually shown up here for eight straight years. Looking back, that was probably a mistake. In just eight years I've given you enough material for twenty years."

He also noted that Congress would probably be sorry to see him go: "You know, the clock is running down on the Republicans in Congress, too. I feel for them. I really do. They've only got seven more months to investigate me. That's a lot of pressure. So little time, so many unanswered questions.

"Now, some of you might think I've been busy writing my memoirs. I'm not concerned about my memoirs, I'm concerned about my résumé. Here's what I've got so far:

" 'Career objective: to stay president.' But being realistic, I would consider an executive position with another country. Of course, I'd prefer to stay within the G-8.

"I'm working hard on this résumé deal. I've been getting a lot of tips on how to write it, mostly from my staff. They really seem to be up on this stuff. They tell me I have to use the active voice for the résumé. You know, things like 'commanded U.S. armed forces,' 'ordered air strikes,' 'served three terms as president.' Hey, everybody embellishes a little. 'Designed, built, and painted Bridge to the Twenty-first Century.' 'Supervised vice president's invention of the Internet.' 'Generated, attracted, heightened, and maintained controversy.'

"Now, I know lately I haven't done a very good job at creating controversy, and I'm sorry for that. You all have so much less to report.

"But let me say to all of you, I have loved these eight years. You know, I read in the history books how other presidents say the White House is like a penitentiary and every motive they have is suspect. Even George Washington complained he was treated like a common thief. I don't know what the heck they're talking about.

"I've had a wonderful time. It's been an honor to serve and fun to laugh. I only wish that we had laughed more these last eight years. Because power is not the most important thing in life, and it only counts for what you use it. I thank you for what you do every day, thank you for all the fun times Hillary and I have had. Keep at it. It's a great country and it deserves our best. Thank you and God bless you."

After the White House Correspondents Association dinner, cast members of *The West Wing* spent part of their day at the White House watching their real-life counterparts. Joe Lockhart even turned over the reins of the daily briefing to his TV counterpart, Allison Janney.

Harking back to that hilarious video that had opened the dinner, in which Lockhart tried to get an answer from *The West Wing* crew to the question "Why are there so many people running down the hallways?" the assembled reporters decided it was time to get the definitive answer.

"I have not spoken to the president about that, but I will get back to you on that," said Janney.

"Is he up yet?" I asked her.

"I believe he is up, Helen, yes."

"Is he doing any work?"

" 'Is he doing any work?' I have no comment."

"Or is he wandering through the halls?"

"He's taking care of the hallway situation."

Reports had surfaced in April 2000 that Joe Lockhart had given up $10 million in stock options of Internet behemoth America Online. When asked about it on April 20, Lockhart responded, "I am not in a position to confirm the numbers because as I worked on my abacus last night, it made me cry. I turned it down for a much more important opportunity to spend each and every afternoon with you all here. And I think I need to readjust my medication."

Clinton may have fudged on a lot of events in his administration, but his golf scorecard? Good grief. In the spring of 2000 he played with fourth-ranked NCAA golfer Bryce Molder, a twenty-one-year-old junior from Georgia Tech.

The two played a round at the Chenal Country Club in Little Rock. Afterward, Molder said playing with the president was "weird. He shot a ninety. At the end of the game, his scorecard said eighty-four."

Molder, by the way, shot ten birdies and an eagle for a career-low score of sixty.

In an interview with the New York *Daily News* published April 7, 2000, Hillary Rodham Clinton noted that she was getting political advice from a master politician: her husband. "When I was getting ready to make my [campaign] announcement, he said, 'I can't believe how nervous I am, and I'm not even doing it myself.' And I said, 'Now you know how I have felt all these years.' "

At the White House briefing on June 12, 2000, press secretary Joe Lockhart confirmed that Clinton planned to visit Nebraska—the only state he had not visited in his eight years in office—before the end of his term. "In the greatest American spirit of saving the best for last, he intends to go to Nebraska before his term ends."

Lockhart dodged the next two questions—Why had it taken so long? And did Clinton have something against Nebraska?

"I'm sticking with 'saving the best for last,'" Lockhart said.

In June 2000, Clinton was on a short trip to Philadelphia and ended up giving an impromptu history lecture. Standing in the room where the Declaration of Independence was signed, he upstaged his appointed tour guide and began spouting off dates and important events in what became a twenty-minute lecture on American history. Finally, his guide offered him a job.

"Mr. Clinton, we're always looking for volunteers," said Martha Aikens, the Park Service employee who was supposed to be showing Clinton around Independence Hall but was instead standing by and listening to him.

Clinton laughed and continued on with a detailed explanation of how the presidency had changed over time, citing actions from Thomas Jefferson and Abraham Lincoln. Jefferson, for example, made the Louisiana Purchase for a sum that equaled the entire federal budget at the time.

"Can you imagine what Congress would say if I said I want to buy a little land but it will only cost $1.8 trillion?" he asked, referring to the current size of the budget. He also gave detailed examples of other changes to the presidency from the time of the Founding Fathers, who had, he said, wanted to ensure a balance of power in the country.

"I think a lot about this," he said after the history lesson.

In late July 2000, Joe Lockhart was questioned early and often on when the Middle East peace talks would end. The long summit between Israeli Prime Minister Ehud Barak and Palestinian leader Yasir Arafat had been going on for several weeks, and the

Republican National Convention was about to begin in Philadelphia. And on another media radar, talk show hostess Kathie Lee Gifford was ending her fifteen-year association with Regis Philbin on their popular TV show *Live with Regis and Kathie Lee.*

As rumors circulated through the press headquarters that President Clinton would wrap up the summit in a few days, Lockhart offered another date:

"There is an informal deadline. All parties want to be available to watch Kathie Lee Gifford's last show on Friday."

While the saga over six-year-old Cuban refugee Elián González played out, an idea was floated that Congress might vote to grant the youngster citizenship. The question at one of the daily White House briefings was whether President Clinton would sign such a document. Little did I know my book *Front Row at the White House* would figure into such an interchange with Joe Lockhart:

Q: Might he sign a bill and say, "I'll sign this but I'll let the courts make the ultimate decision"?

Lockhart: I wouldn't get into a "might" or an "if" here. I was just . . . to tell you the truth, I was just reading a very interesting segment of Helen's book yesterday while I was going through, and it has a section in there where my predecessor [Mike McCurry] talked about "only fools answer hypotheticals," so I will not be foolish today.

Helen: Well, I have a hypothetical. . . .

Lockhart: Helen, what is the name of your publisher again?

As the first couple made their move to their new home in Chappaqua, New York, Mrs. Clinton noted that the president handles moving the furniture "and I tell him where to move it."

And like most husbands, he also put himself in charge of the TV remote.

"I think that's also genetic, the male DNA," she said. "I think when we finally map the human genome, we're going to find these tiny little strands that say 'moving,' 'never ask for directions,' and 'the remote'—all on the man."

When the first lady decided to run for the Senate seat in New York, President Clinton spoke in early September 2000 at a fund-raiser and noted, "For apart from this extraordinary personal feeling about this race, the reason I'm going around the country now—the first time in twenty-six years when I haven't been on the ballot during an election—is because I've worked as hard as I could to turn our country around and move it in the right direction.

"But I honestly believe all the best things are still out there. And I think this is the first time in my lifetime that our nation has had a chance to shed its baggage, to shed its racial baggage, to shed its homophobic baggage, to shed all of its divisive baggage. My party has shed a lot of that baggage that basically was rooted in our fear of change and has embraced change."

Much was made of Al Gore's choice of Senator Joseph Lieberman of Connecticut to be his running mate, and even Clinton weighed in at a reception for Representative Dennis Moore of Kansas in October: "Actually, I was thinking that I kind of resented that Al Gore has gotten all this credit—for naming Joe Lieberman to the ticket. I mean, I know it's a big deal to have the first Jewish vice presidential nominee.

"But I mean, come on now, look at American history—that is nothing compared to the first Jewish Agriculture Secretary [Dan Glickman]. I mean, just with a decision I destroyed one of the great stereotypes in American life—nobody thinks *Jewish farmer* is an oxymoron anymore."

On September 29, 2000, Joe Lockhart became the fourth press secretary to leave the Clinton White House. His last briefing was hilarious, touching, and nostalgic. And of course, his staff was not above inserting a few practical jokes. At one point, Lockhart took a sip of water from a glass underneath the podium:

Lockhart: Who did this? Okay, I'm not moving, I'm not touching anything.

Q: Vodka or gin?

Lockhart: Vodka, I believe. (Laughter) Yes?

Q: Can you take that?

Lockhart: I don't even remember what the question was.

A short time later, chief of staff John Podesta and President Clinton entered the pressroom, and Podesta demanded, "We want the podium."

"Oh, *you* want the podium?" Lockhart responded, then saw Clinton standing behind Podesta. "Oh."

Podesta: You know, here in the White House, we're obviously sorry to see Joe leave us. But I have to tell you all that the same ain't true for the Republicans. Just this morning, in [House Majority Whip] Tom DeLay's favorite newspaper, Joe is described as the "fiercely partisan White House press secretary." (Laughter) Let me tell you, they want him out of here. (Laughter) It's not just that Joe is better at driving the Republicans crazy than just about anybody. It's that Joe gets results for the American people. Just yesterday Joe was here whacking them for failing to get their work done. And you know what? It worked. They're so tired of hearing Joe label them a "do-nothing Congress" that last night the Senate finally passed twenty-four bills. Now, it's true, they still haven't raised the minimum wage or passed a patients' bill of rights, but Joe finally kicked them into gear. Last night they passed the FHA Down Payment Simplification Extension Act of 2000. I know there are a lot of people who aren't usually in these briefings here, so for those of you who don't know what that is, that's simply an extension of the FHA Down Payment Simplification Act of 2000. So we still don't have a Medicare prescription-drug benefit, but thanks to Joe's bully pulpit, we have S893, a bill to amend Title 46, United States Code, to provide equitable treatment with respect to certain individuals who perform duties on vessels. Thank you, Joe.

One reporter noted, "That's good. You ought to keep him on and see what else he can do."

"That's a really bad idea," Lockhart responded.

Podesta went on to note that Congress had also passed "one measure of some significance yesterday that had nothing to do with pressure from Joe. They passed HR4931, the Presidential Transition Act of 2000. Of course, the only reason the Republicans passed that was because it authorizes funds to move the president out of the White House. [Laughter] I think it's fair to say, for those of us on the White House staff, that if we got to vote a bill to keep Joe in the White House, that vote would have passed by unanimous consent. He's been tough, he's been funny, he's always been straight. I think I said to the staff this morning, I think you can't count on one hand the times that Joe has made a mistake here, despite the fact that you guys throw him fastballs on a day-in-and-day-out basis."

Podesta then introduced Clinton, who began, "Most people think Joe's leaving for purely selfish, monetary reasons. But the truth is, he told me that I was no longer in enough trouble to make it interesting for him. That getting up every day and going to work and making policy and helping the Democrats, you know, it's boring him to tears. And he said he couldn't stand to be alone in his office crying anymore, and so he had to leave. So I have one little gift to him, a memorial of our one and only day playing golf together. It happened a couple of weeks ago."

Clinton then gave Lockhart a picture with the caption "Joe's typical day as presidential press secretary, lost in the weeds. Unlike the press corps, I'll give you a mulligan."

The president ended his remarks: "Let me say seriously, I know what a difficult job this is, and I know it takes a toll on everyone, and I know Joe's spent a lot of time away from his wonderful wife and beautiful daughter, who are here. I remember when I appointed him, there was all this yapping about whether he was heavy enough to do the job. He leaves with gravitas and gravy toss. And a lot of gratitude. I know that I have a different perspective than the members of the press corps, but I've been following this business a long time, a long time before I showed up. I don't believe I've ever seen anybody do this job better. I admire you. I'm grateful to you. I'll miss you—and I'll try to keep you bored. Thank you, friend."

Lockhart's response to his boss: "You don't have to hang around for this part. You don't really want to talk to them. I'm still on the clock."

"You want us to go?" said Clinton. "Well, wait, I've got to do one thing. I have a gift for your successor, Jake [Siewert]." Clinton produced a helmet with Jake's name on it. "They're going to try to get even with you, and they're also going to try to get even for everything they couldn't get away with with Joe, so I thought you ought to have this. I hope you'll wear it to your first briefing."

And the new press secretary replied, "I worked enough on the Dukakis campaign not to put this on."

Clinton: Joe?

Lockhart: No, I won't put it on.

After Clinton left, Lockhart was peppered with questions about what he would be doing to earn a living, and someone recalled his appearance in the video at the White House Correspondents dinner, in which Lockhart spoke to *The West Wing* cast members on the set, asking each of them why the series always showed "so many people walking around the hallways."

Q: Joe, is it true, now that you're gone, you're going to have a recurring role on *The West Wing*?

Lockhart: They have enough hapless people already, they don't need me.

Q: Have they asked you?

Lockhart: No, they have not. I have enormous respect for what they do, I like their program. They even sent me something nice as a going-away present.

Q: What?

Lockhart: A director's chair, with my name on it. It's very nice.

Then there was the question we all wanted to ask:

Q: Joe, how really did the press treat you, and how did you like the press?

Lockhart: Do you want an honest answer?

Q: Yes.

Lockhart: No, we won't do that. No, that's a good question. Let me take an opportunity to try to answer it.

I remember on my first day when I came in, Helen Thomas grabbed me and, with a knowing smile, said, "You're feeling pretty good about this today, aren't you?" And I said, "Well, I think so. I've wanted to do this for some time. I'm going to get to do it. I'm a little nervous, but I think it will be okay." She said, "Enjoy these briefings. You're going to come to hate them. Every press secretary does. It's an albatross. You're going to hate it."

And for once, I think I've been able to prove Helen wrong, and that's enough for my career. I have never stopped enjoying coming down here. I've lost some of my desire for all the preparation it takes to come down here and talk to you all, but I've never not enjoyed coming down and facing this back-and-forth. It has been fun, it has been a pleasure to work with each and every one of you. I think—I hope we have demonstrated a commitment and demonstrated that we understand what you do and we value what you do. And I leave probably having had cross words with everyone in the room, but we have had very positive conversations. And I thank all of you for that.

Then, rather than giving the press corps the usual "week ahead"—the White House releases a tentative presidential schedule on Friday of the next week's events—Lockhart gave us his own personal "week ahead" for his first days off the job:

"I just looked down at this and realized that, in addition to the drink under here, they've [the staff] also had some fun with the week ahead. So, here goes. It turns out that this is not the week ahead for the schedule of the president, it is the week ahead for the schedule for me.

"Saturday, September 30, down until 2 P.M. No public schedule, but there is a photo release. It is Joe Lockhart shaking hands with Rick Lazio [Hillary Rodham Clinton's opposition in the race for the New York Senate seat]. Who knew they could find that?

"Sunday, October 1, attend confession, ask forgiveness for all that lying to [AP White House correspondent] Terry Hunt.

"Monday, October 2, arrive at Elizabeth Arden Salon for deep-tissue massage, seaweed wrap, salt glow, and pedicure. Five P.M., meet the mole at the private residence at the Watergate Hotel.

"Tuesday, October 3, 9 A.M., interview candidates for my own personal Tae Bo trainer. Afternoon, attend first meeting of Spinners Anonymous.

"Wednesday, October 4, shave.

"Thursday, October 5, 10 A.M., speech to Dallas oilmen's club. Two P.M., speech to Pharmaceutical Manufacturers Association. Five P.M., speech to the National Association of HMOs. Eight P.M., pick up new Ferrari at dealership.

"Friday, seminar at the Brookings Institution, entitled 'Art of the Apology in the Modern Political World.' I will be representing the president. Other guests include Howell Raines and Jeff Gerth.

"And finally, Saturday, I'm going to Disney World. And I'm done. Thank you very much."

* * *

At the opening ceremonies of the 2000 President's Cup in October at the Robert Trent Jones Golf Course in Lake Manassas, Virginia, Clinton told those assembled, "As a gesture of goodwill, I left my clubs home today. Actually, I offered to play on the American team, but when I had to confess I have never broken eighty on this course—even on the white tees—I was immediately rejected, showing how much the world has changed since President Johnson said, 'There's one lesson you better learn if you want to be in politics: never go out on a golf course and beat the president.' I keep passing that out, even to strangers, and no one takes it seriously anymore.

"Now, as honorary chairman, my first order of business is to declare this tournament officially open. Secondly, I have been informed—much against my better instincts—to declare this a no-mulligan zone."

In November 2000, the popular Los Angeles deejay Jay Thomas and Bill Clinton posed for a picture during a fund-raiser. Thomas said to Clinton, "I already have two shots of me standing next to a cardboard cutout of you."

Clinton responded, "After this one, tell me which one is livelier."

At a "Get Out the Vote" rally in New York in early November, Clinton gave the crowd his take on the "fuzzy math" phrase that was peppering the Gore-Bush presidential race: "Now look, here's the problem. You all clapped for me when I said the economy was better. But people ask me all the time, what great new idea did you bring to Washington to turn the economy around? You know what I answer? Arithmetic. We brought arithmetic back to Washington."

* * *

November 9, 2000, was one of Washington's most historic nights at the White House, and I was honored to be among those attending the dinner celebrating the two hundredth anniversary of the White House.

Even with all the campaign brouhaha swirling around, President and Mrs. Clinton staged a memorable dinner with a few guests I'd also been acquainted with: Lady Bird Johnson, Gerald and Betty Ford, Jimmy and Rosalynn Carter, and George and Barbara Bush. Clinton's toast that night:

"It has been said that an invitation to the White House to dinner is one of the highest compliments a president can bestow on anyone. Tonight Hillary and I would amend that to say that an even higher compliment has been bestowed on us by your distinguished presence this evening. In the entire two hundred years of the White House history, never before have this many former presidents and first ladies gathered in this great room.

"Hillary and I are grateful beyond words to have served as temporary stewards of the People's House these last eight years, an honor exceeded only by the privilege of service that comes with the key to the front door.

"In the short span of two hundred years, those whom the wings of history have brought to this place have shaped not only their own times, but have also left behind a living legacy for our own. In ways both large and small, each and every one of you has cast your light upon this house and left it and our country brighter for it. For that, Hillary and I and all Americans owe you a great debt of gratitude.

"I salute you and all those yet to grace these halls with the words of the very first occupant of the White House, John Adams, who said, 'I pray to heaven to bestow the best of blessings on this house, and all that shall hereafter inhabit it. May none but the honest and wise rule under this roof.'

"Ladies and gentlemen, I ask you to join me in a toast to Mrs.

Johnson, President and Mrs. Ford, President and Mrs. Carter, President and Mrs. Bush, for their honest and wise service to the people while they inhabited this house."

Clinton also didn't miss the opportunity to remark that all the presidents who attended the two hundredth anniversary dinner "have been around for half as much as Helen Thomas."

In a column she later wrote about the evening, Hillary Rodham Clinton remarked that it "would have been an extraordinary evening even under ordinary circumstances. But given these times, these four presidents—Democrats and Republicans alike—reminded us of the power of our democracy to endure and thrive."

Each president that evening was invited to deliver remarks. Gerald Ford was the first to speak. "Once again," he said, "the world's oldest republic has demonstrated the youthful vitality of its institutions and the ability and the necessity to come together after a hard-fought campaign. The clash of partisan political ideas does remain just that—to be quickly followed by a peaceful transfer of authority."

Ford also talked about how it was impossible to walk the halls of the White House without being touched by the lives of all who had come before and how he was "humbled by the inescapable presence of my predecessors—Jackson, Lincoln, the two Roosevelts, Truman and Eisenhower, and so many others who live in our imagination and our idealism."

Jimmy Carter said, "The White House epitomizes for all Americans the stability and the greatness of peace and freedom and democracy and human rights not only for all Americans, but for all people in the world. And my dream is that the epitome of the high ideals of humankind expressed in physical terms in the White House will continue for another hundred or even a thousand years."

Carter and Ford both noted that during their hard-fought 1976 campaign, neither could have predicted the close relationship that they enjoy today. In fact, at a press conference earlier in the day, Carter was asked whether he found it strange that he and Clinton would be attending an event with Gerald Ford and George Bush. "I think that's a vivid demonstration of what the White House and service in it means to all of us," he replied.

When it came time for George Bush to speak, he referred to the still unsettled presidential election and the timeless quality of the house: "For two hundred years and eight days, this old house had been buffeted by the winds of change and battered by the troubled waters of war. We've been favored by calm seas, too. But history tells us a democracy thrives when the gusts and gales of challenge and adversity fill its sails and compel it into action. And through it all, through trial and tribulation, as well as triumph, the White House has served as our nation's anchor to windward, a vision of constancy, a fortress of freedom, the repository of a billion American dreams. Age and the elements occasionally wear her down, but this house is forever renewed by the ageless fidelity of its founders, and the boundless promise of its future heirs."

In his last days in office, Clinton was featured in a film giving a White House tour, part of a documentary that will be shown at his presidential library.

The director was none other than Wes Craven, the man behind such slasher films as *Scream* and *Nightmare on Elm Street*. That of course had people wondering what the title of the Clinton film would be: *Nightmare on Pennsylvania Avenue?*

"I was thinking, 'Here I am. I've made some of the most horrific films, and now I'm in the White House,'" Craven said. "Someone said I should have brought a *Scream* mask and have someone jump out in it, but that would have been the last time we would have been invited over."

* * *

When Clinton was preparing to leave office in January 2001, the White House staff decided to come up with yet another "week ahead" schedule that rivaled the one they had put together for Joe Lockhart.

Jake Siewert got to do the honors of describing the president's final few days in office at a regular briefing:

Q: Jake, how is the president going to spend the last night in the White House?

Siewert: I think he's going to be packing, seeing his family. He's got a little work to do this afternoon. He may make some calls just to thank people around the world for the work that they've done together.

Q: He's not finished packing?

Siewert: He has not finished packing. I have, almost. But I keep getting mail, though.

Q: Jake, can you give us a sense of the chronology tomorrow [Inauguration Day], what the president is going to be doing before noontime?

Siewert: President and Mrs. Clinton will meet with the president-elect and Mrs. Bush here in the morning around ten-twenty, at the White House. They'll have coffee, an informal coffee, I think in the Blue Room. They'll then proceed via motorcade together to the Capitol, where he will witness the inaugural ceremony. At that point, he will leave and head to Andrews, where he has a ceremony—approximately one-thirty or so at Andrews. He'll fly to New York after that. Then there's an event planned in New York around three for his arrival there to welcome him home. At that point, he'll fly on helicopter up to Chappaqua and spend the night with his family.

Q: Will he be saying good-bye? Will there be any sort of ceremony where he says good-bye to White House staff?

Siewert: The staff are all invited to Andrews. And you're also welcome, as well—it's open press—if you don't have anything else to do.

After more questions about the president's plans, Siewert launched into a long thank-you to the many staff members "who day in and day out work to help you cover the president. It's been a long and arduous eight years," and he then thanked the press corps "for making our time here memorable."

I then thanked him for "standing in the hottest spot in the world," but he wasn't quite done. After mentioning more names, Siewert noted, "And I have a week ahead," detailing the ex-president's schedule, and gave us a rundown of Clinton's activities:

Sunday, January 21, 1 P.M.: set up new E-mail account, waspotus@aol.com. That will be closed to the press.

Monday, January 22, from 9 A.M. to 4 P.M.: The president will be awaiting the arrival of the Westchester County cable guy. That is also closed to the press.

Tuesday, January 23, from 9 A.M. to 4 P.M.: He will be awaiting the arrival of the Westchester cable guy.

On Wednesday, January 24, the president is going to pitch DreamWorks guys on movie treatment: Lithuanian terrorists capture Air Force One, president ends hostage situation by negotiating $3.2 billion debt-forgiveness package and micro-credit loan guarantees for Lithuania.

Saturday, January 27, 11 A.M.: Depart for Mount Kisco Pep Boys to purchase timing belt and spark plugs for 1968 Mustang. Pool press hopefully. If anyone still cares then.

And also on Saturday, January 27, the president will deliver—10:10 A.M.—will deliver the Democratic response to President Bush's radio address.

At a regular briefing shortly before Clinton left office, Siewert was also asked whether Clinton appointees will have to be swept out of their offices by the new administration. "We'll leave," he said. "They don't need to clear us out, we're happy to go."

Joe Lockhart also showed up that day to make a cameo appearance. Siewert noted that Lockhart "offered to brief, but I told him it wasn't necessary. He's gone through enough suffering up here."

More brouhahas were brewing for the first couple after the president left office. Senator Hillary Rodham Clinton signed an $8 million deal with Simon & Schuster to write her memoirs, and then there was that pesky financial disclosure form that showed an estimated $190,000 worth of gifts received the previous year. The report ran seven pages, detailing furniture to china to flatware to a set of boxing gloves from actor Sylvester Stallone to a copy of President Abraham Lincoln's Cooper Union speech worth $9,683 from insurance magnate Walter Kaye—who had lobbied to get Monica Lewinsky her White House internship.

Yet another congressional panel was convened to examine the largess. Sheila Tate, Nancy Reagan's White House press secretary—who knew her way around home-furnishing flaps, given Nancy's bad press when she was first lady—said she had never heard of anything like it: "These are not the kind of gifts you take with you. It's usually a silver bowl with your name on it."

In all of the frenzy about the Clintons' "raiding" the White House to furnish their two homes, little did I know how prophetic one of my questions was. I remembered something he said to me on one of his last trips to Lansing, Michigan. Everyone had been clamoring for an end-of-administration interview, and since I'm well acquainted with the time it takes to fly from Washington to Michigan, I asked for a few minutes of his time on that trip. When I finally got admitted to his quarters, we had a pretty run-of-the-mill session about his legacy, what his hopes were for the country, that kind of thing.

Then I asked him, "Mr. President, if there was one thing you could take with you from the White House that belongs to the American people, what would it be?"

He said it would be the moon rock that Neil Armstrong had brought back when men walked on the moon in 1969. He said the rock, which was kept on a table in the Oval Office, helped to put everything in perspective.

"When everybody was running around or got upset about something," he said, he would tell them to "remember the rock. It's 3.6 billion years old. We're all just passing through, and we need to chill out here and make the most of the moment."

A first-rate item from the New York *Daily News,* February 1, 2001: "Bill Clinton is finding out just how blasé New Yorkers can be about him. After the former president took in the St. John's–UConn game on Tuesday, he went to Babbo for dinner with former Senator Bob Kerrey of Nebraska and four others. As two other people were leaving the West Village restaurant, one turned to the other and said, 'That poor guy, looking so much like Bill Clinton. His life must be hell.' "

Do some things turn out for the best? After the big flap about the former president considering renting high-priced office space in the Carnegie Towers on West Fifty-seventh Street, it turned out that if he had, Clinton and a former White House intern would have been answering to the same landlord. Carnegie Towers landlord Rockrose is also the management company of record at the Greenwich Village apartment house where Monica Lewinsky lives.

Reports in March 2001 indicated that Bartlett's *Familiar Quotations* would be adding three entries courtesy of ex-President Clinton. They are:

"I experimented with marijuana a time or two. And I didn't

like it, and didn't inhale and I never tried it again." *New York Times,* March 31, 1992.

"I am going to say this again: I did not have sexual relations with that woman, Miss Lewinsky." Televised speech, January 26, 1998.

"It depends on what the meaning of *is* is. If the—if he—if *is* means and never has been—that is not—that is one thing. If it means there is none, that was a completely true statement." Grand jury testimony, August 17, 1998.

As the New York *Daily News* aptly described it, "It's Not the Heat, It's the Humidor." In late March 2001 the former president was honored at the Italian embassy for his administration's work to help victims of brain injuries. As a token of appreciation, Clinton was presented with a humidor. Harking back to the Monica Lewinsky scandal and stories of cigars as sex toys, the room got uncomfortably quiet. However, Clinton must have taken it all in stride. He reportedly walked into a cigar shop at London's Heathrow Airport several days later and bought a Cuban cigar. "He has been given humidors and cigars before," said his spokeswoman, Julia Payne. "I realize the double entendre, but this is not something his friends have stopped giving him."

At his last White House Correspondents Association dinner, Clinton remarked that he would likely come down with a condition common to former presidents: AGDD—Attention Getting Deficit Disorder.

It's not likely that will occur anytime soon, but on a trip to Ireland in late May 2001, he was greeted with boos from protesters. But he didn't mind. He said it was a sign of a healthy democracy that "people have a right to be wrong and loudly wrong." Besides, he added, "Nobody demonstrates against me anymore. This is fun. You guys better be careful. I might think I was still president."

* * *

President Clinton gave his first speech in Washington since leaving office on June 28, 2001, at an event sponsored by the John F. Kennedy School of Government, on the role of race and the press.

"I am, I think, glad to be back," the ex-president told an audience of more than two hundred members of the media, academics, and policymakers.

He spotted me in the audience and noted, "Helen, you can ask me a question when it's over. I can say that because nobody cares what my answer is anymore."

Clinton was back in Washington in the late fall of 2001 as the first speaker in the Nation's Capital Distinguished Speaker series, sponsored by the Greater Washington Society of Association Executives.

It was a packed house that night, with every one of the 2,200 seats filled at the Kennedy Center, where the event took place. I had the pleasure of introducing the former president and noted that President Bush was fortunate to have the surplus that the Clinton administration had left behind, so he could pay some bills the nation would be facing since the September 11 terrorist attacks.

I went on to say that each person in the audience probably was looking forward to Clinton's memoirs and further noted a habit among readers in Washington—that we especially looked forward to the index to see whether our names were included.

Clinton walked onto the stage and in his opening remarks leaned my way and said not to worry. "Your name will be listed in the index several times."

Then he faced the audience and said that while he enjoyed listening to my introduction, something else had been on his mind: "All I could think was 'I hope she doesn't ask me a question.'"

GEORGE W. BUSH

It is enough that the people know there was an election. The people who cast the votes decide nothing. The people who count the votes decide everything.

—JOSEPH STALIN

George W. Bush came to the White House with a reputation as an English mangler, an expert at malapropisms—who somehow is fluent in Spanish. (Yeah, right.)

On the campaign trail the Greeks were the "Grecians" and "Is our children learning?" was emblazoned on protest posters to remind us that Bush had somehow skipped English 101.

But he is the only president we've got, as LBJ liked to point out about himself.

In the presidency, where almost everything is written for you, Bush managed to get by a little better with English as his first language. But he has provided a lot of fodder with his extemporaneous flubs.

He also has provided some fun with his nicknames for members of the press. He nicknamed *New York Times* columnist Maureen Dowd "Cobra," and for her, it turned into a good column. I was asked in an interview if I had any idea what I'd been tagged with. "I don't know what he calls me, but I can imagine," I said.

George W. was the family cutup. He was president of his fraternity at Yale, and it seemed to be all fun and games for him. When he returned to Yale in the spring of 2001 during his first year as president to receive an honorary degree, he jokingly told C-average students they, too, could be president.

Funny thing, Americans never give presidential candidates an IQ test. But they seem to put a lot of stock in a sense of humor and quick wit.

The Gore-Bush stories came from everywhere in the last election. From Australia's *Sydney Morning Herald*: "There's a pleasant little walking track between Wollstonecraft and Greenwich," says Jim McSharry, of Wollstonecraft. "It runs beside Gore Creek and it's called the Gore Bush Track. That's logical because it doesn't go anywhere."

TV headline from Florida, November 28, 2000: "Florida certifies George W. Bush . . . and a tennis ball explodes, killing a dog."

On January 2, 2001, at a White House briefing, press secretary Ari Fleischer made note that the Bush White House had received forty-two thousand résumés.

To which I responded, "Well, how come you can count those but you can't count the ballots?"

As the Bush team worked to assemble its picks for White House posts in late November, people speculated that some Wyoming pols might be considered plum picks. Former Republican Senator Alan K. Simpson, however, made it clear that he would not be one of them. Simpson, who is teaching at the University of Wyoming in Laramie, told his class, "The answer is not 'no.' It is 'hell no.' There will be Wyoming people in this administration, but I will only be senior geezer counselor," said the sixty-nine-year-old former senator, who served from 1979 to 1997. Still, he had some fond memories of his Senate days. "How about throwing snowballs off the roof of the White House with George Bush after a couple of beers?" he said. "Actually," he corrected himself, "it was a fine red wine."

In the middle of the election brouhaha down in Florida, every hotel room in Tallahassee was occupied. However, Florida had its priorities. One weekend the media were told they had to get out of their rooms, as the University of Florida–Florida State football game was scheduled and all the rooms had been prebooked for months in advance. Some enterprising locals put up signs— "Need a Place to Stay?"—even in the courtyard of the Capitol in a bid to cash in on the political overdrive.

Bill Cotterell was in the middle of it all with his reporting duties and noted that "every news event is a mob scene— microphone booms hanging overhead, people shouting all at once. Walk through the courtyard and you'll hear every language known. We had a tornado alert this morning but none hit. I was hoping if it *had* to hit, it'd come right down Adams Street, through the Capitol."

He also noted that by city ordinance, office buildings, stores, and restaurants were limited to two stories within a few blocks of the Capitol so it stands out, and some networks leased space on top of the nearby buildings "so our rather unusual Capitol looms in the background. For those who've never seen it all, the Florida Capitol is a twenty-two-story tower with domes over the House and Senate office buildings at the sixth-floor level on either side of the shaft. Yes, that's exactly what it looks like. . . . Many newcomers think they're the first to notice this. Others say, '*What* were they thinking?' "

As the election-that-never-seemed-to-end was about to begin, I gave a speech at the Associated Press Managing Editors annual conference in San Antonio and noted that whether it would be Al Gore or George W. Bush, there was one activity I could do without.

"Whoever wins, I hope he doesn't jog. I know that's a vain hope, but getting up at the crack of dawn to watch a president in his running shorts is not my idea of fun."

The many, many campaign "Bushisms" are part of political lore now. Even during the budget battles right before the 106th Congress adjourned, Senator Harry Reid, Democrat of Nevada, filling time on the floor, read a number of them into the *Congressional Record:*

"How do you know if you don't measure, if you have a system that simply suckles kids through?" Explaining the need for educational accountability in Beaufort, South Carolina, February 16, 2000.

"Will the highways on the Internet become more few?" Concord, New Hampshire, January 29, 2000.

"This is Preservation Month. I appreciate preservation. It's what you do when you run for president. You gotta preserve." Speaking during "Perseverance Month" at Fairgrounds Elementary School in Nashua, New Hampshire. As quoted in the *Los Angeles Times,* January 28, 2000.

"I know how hard it is for you to put food on your family." Greater Nashua, New Hampshire, Chamber of Commerce, January 27, 2000.

"What I am against is quotas. I am against hard quotas, quotas they basically delineate based upon whatever. However they delineate. Quotas, I think, vulcanize society. So, I don't know how that fits into what everybody else is saying, their relative positions, but that's my position." Quoted by Molly Ivins, *San Francisco Chronicle,* January 21, 2000.

"When I was coming up, it was a dangerous world, and you knew exactly who they were. It was us versus them, and it was clear who them was. Today we are not so sure who the they are, but we know they're there." Iowa Western Community College, January 21, 2000.

"The administration I'll bring is a group of men and women who are focused on what's best for America, honest men and women, decent men and women, women who will not stain the House." *Des Moines Register* debate, Iowa, January 15, 2000.

"This is still a dangerous world. It's a world of madmen and uncertainty and potential mental losses." At a South Carolina oyster roast, as quoted in the *Financial Times,* January 14, 2000.

"Rarely is the question asked: Is our children learning?" Florence, South Carolina, January 11, 2000.

"There needs to be debates, like we're going through. There needs to be town-hall meetings. There needs to be travel. This is a huge country." *Larry King Live,* December 16, 1999.

"The important question is, How many hands have I shaked?" Answering a question about why he hadn't spent more time in New Hampshire, in the *New York Times,* October 23, 1999.

"It was just inebriating what Midland was all about then." From a 1994 interview, as quoted in *First Son* by Bill Minutaglio.

"An increasing amount of our imports are coming from overseas." *NPR Morning Edition,* September 26, 2000.

"Actually, I—this may sound a little West Texan to you, but I like it. When I'm talking about—when I'm talking about myself, and when he's talking about myself, all of us are talking about me." *Hardball,* MSNBC, May 31, 2000.

"It's clearly a budget. It's got a lot of numbers in it." Reuters, May 5, 2000.

"I think we agree, the past is over." On his meeting with John McCain, *Dallas Morning News,* May 10, 2000.

"Laura and I really don't realize how bright our children is sometime until we get an objective analysis." *Meet the Press,* April 15, 2000.

"I was raised in the West. The west of Texas. It's pretty close to California. In more ways than Washington, D.C., is close to California." *Los Angeles Times,* April 8, 2000.

"We want our teachers to be trained so they can meet the obligations, their obligations as teachers. We want them to know how to teach the science of reading. In order to make sure there's not this kind of federal cufflink." Fritsche Middle School, Milwaukee, March 30, 2000.

"The fact that he relies on facts—says things that are not factual—are going to undermine his campaign." *New York Times,* March 4, 2000.

"It is not Reaganesque to support a tax plan that is Clinton in nature." Los Angeles, February 23, 2000.

"I understand small business growth. I was one." New York *Daily News,* February 19, 2000.

"The senator has got to understand he can't have it both ways. He can't take the high horse and then claim the low road." To reporters in Florence, South Carolina, February 17, 2000.

"If you're sick and tired of the politics of cynicism and polls and principles, come and join this campaign." Hilton Head, South Carolina, February 16, 2000.

"We ought to make the pie higher." South Carolina Republican Debate, February 15, 2000.

"I've changed my style somewhat, as you know. I'm less, I pontificate less, although it may be hard to tell it from this show. And I'm more interacting with people." *Meet the Press,* February 13, 2000.

"I think we need not only to eliminate the tollbooth to the middle class, I think we should knock down the tollbooth." Nashua, New Hampshire, as quoted by Gail Collins, *New York Times,* February 1, 2000.

"The most important job is not to be governor, or first lady in my case." Pella, Iowa, as quoted in the *San Antonio Express News,* January 30, 2000.

"We must all hear the universal call to like your neighbor

just like you like to be liked yourself." At a South Carolina oyster roast, as quoted in the *Financial Times,* January 14, 2000.

"Keep good relations with the Grecians." Quoted in the *Economist,* June 12, 1999.

"I think anybody who doesn't think I'm smart enough to handle the job is underestimating." *U.S. News & World Report,* April 3, 2000.

In May 2000, Bush was appearing at the New Media Seminar in New York and glanced at a tape copy of *Running Mates,* a political comedy, starring Tom Selleck and Faye Dunaway, that appeared on the TNT cable channel.

"Oh, *Running Mates,*" said Bush. "Maybe I should watch that before choosing one."

Shortly after the inauguration, President Bush went to work on his economic plan. However, changing the currency was not part of the game plan. Still, that didn't stop someone in Danville, Kentucky, who managed to pay for a $2 order at a fast-food restaurant with a bogus $200 bill featuring a picture of the president and an illustration of the White House with a sign in front that said "We like broccoli" (harking back to his father's admitted dislike for the vegetable), and on the back, a picture of an oil well.

Police said the cashier at the Dairy Queen even gave the culprit $198 in real money as change.

I took some heat for a remark at the White House when President-elect Bush visited with President Clinton after the election.

I asked Clinton whether he still planned to go to North Korea, and he said no decision had been made, at which point I asked Bush, "Governor, you're not against him going, is that right?"

Bush: I haven't had a chance to talk to the president yet, Helen.

Clinton: We've got to talk about this.

Helen: What will you tell him is the biggest problem, Mr. President?

Clinton: I want to talk to him, not you. He can talk about that. I waited eight years to say that.

President-elect Bush went on to say that it was a "huge honor" to arrive at the White House as the president-elect and he was "humbled and honored, and I can't thank the president enough for his hospitality—he didn't need to do this."

"Yes, he did," I piped up. "It's protocol."

Bush: I hadn't quite finished yet.

Helen: Go ahead and finish.

Bush: And I'm grateful. And I look forward to the discussion; I'm here to listen. And if the president is kind enough to offer some advice, if he is, I will take it.

Helen: Are there questions you have for the president, sir?

Bush: If there are, I'm going to ask it in private—and afterwards not share them with you.

Later in the day, an anchor on CNBC remarked, "Well, as you just heard, the president-elect was just baptized into the White House press corps by Helen Thomas."

I spoke to students and faculty at Lynn University in Florida on January 18, 2001 and was asked a question about how the new first lady, Laura Bush, saw her role. I said that she, like mother-in-law Barbara Bush, probably would not buck the Washington establishment and that both women likely would continue with their reading and literacy projects.

"You know," I added, "none of this seems to rub off on the prominent men in their family."

At the Alfalfa Club dinner on January 27, 2001, a week after the inauguration, Bush's sense of humor about much that had been written about him began to emerge as fodder for speeches. "I want to clear something up right at the start," he told the crowd.

"I know there are those of you here tonight who doubt my leadership ability. They question my intellectual depth. To those people I can say but one thing: you're my family and I love you. By the way, my three brothers—Jeb, Neil, and Marvin—are here. But as I told Dick Cheney during the transition, 'In this administration there is no room for nepotism or any other word I don't understand.'"

On another family note—and many family members were at the dinner—Bush said he was using one of the desks his father had had in his administration, "and the first time I opened the drawer, there was a letter from him addressed to me and dated when he was still president. You can imagine the emotion I felt as I read: 'Dear George, I just knew that you would someday end up in the White House. I am so proud of you. Love, Dad.

" 'P.S. Give my regards to President Cheney and Vice President McCain.'"

At his first Gridiron dinner on March 24, 2001, Bush hit on his intellectual acumen again. He said he thought he had pretty good relations with "you all in the press. However, those stories about my intellectual capacity do get under my skin a bit. For a while, I thought even my own staff believed them. There on my schedule first thing every morning, it said, 'Intelligence briefing.' At one point, I even called Robert Strauss and asked him how I should deal with this perception I wasn't up to the job. He said, 'Just remember, Mr. President, you can fool some of the people all of the time—and those are the people you need to concentrate on.' You know what Garrison Keillor said the other day? He said that 'George Bush's lips are where words go to die.'"

Bush continues to poke fun at himself and his fractured way of speaking in his speeches. At the Radio-Television Correspondents Association dinner on March 29, 2001, he even revisited some of the gaffe lines from the campaign and did his best to explain them. A book had recently been published on the "accidental wit and wisdom" of George W. Bush, and he said, "I'm kind of proud that my words are already in book form, so, like other authors, I thought I'd read from it tonight. It's like *The Thoughts of Chairman Mao*—only with laughs and not in Chinese.

"Here's one, and I actually said this: 'I know the human being and fish can coexist peacefully.' Now, *that* makes you stop and think. Anyone can give you a coherent sentence, but something like this takes you into an entirely new dimension.

"Here's another: 'I understand small business growth. I was one.' I love great literature.

"I said this up in New Hampshire: 'I appreciate preservation. It's what you do when you run for president. You gotta preserve.' I don't have the slightest idea what I was talking about there.

"Now, most people would say, in speaking of the economy, 'We ought to make the pie bigger.' I, however, am on record saying, 'We ought to make the pie higher.' It's a very complicated economic point I was making there, but believe me, what this country needs is a taller pie.

"Then there is the famous 'Rarely is the question asked: Is our children learning?' Let's analyze that sentence for a moment. If you're a stickler, you probably think the singular verb *is* should have been the plural *are.* But if you read it closely, you'll see that I'm using the intransitive plural subjunctive tense and so the word *is* are correct.

"Finally, let's see you wordsmiths out there diagram this sentence, and I quote: 'This may sound a little West Texas to you, but when I'm talking about myself, and when he's talking about myself, all of us are talking about me.' Ladies and gentlemen, you have to admit in my sentences, I go where no man has gone before."

In his closing he noted, "I don't think it's too healthy to take yourself too seriously. But what I do take seriously is my responsibility as president to all of the American people and to the office that I hold. And that is what I came tonight to tell you.

"Thank you for inviting me and thank you for your kind horse-pitality."

At the swearing-in ceremony for Agriculture Secretary Ann M. Veneman, Bush noted, "Ann and I will carry out this equivocal message to the world: Markets must be open."

Speaking about the first lady, Bush said of his wife, Laura, "I have the best wife for the line of work that I'm in. She doesn't try to steal the limelight."

I got to do a little of my own joking about the Bush father-and-son syntactic tag team at the Gridiron in March 2000. With George W. coming on strong as the GOP presidential contender and his slips of speech making their way into the press every day, the songwriters came up with lyrics for me to the tune of "Why Can't the English (Teach Their Children How to Speak?)" from the musical *My Fair Lady*. There I stood onstage, decked out in Barbara Bush pearls and a Barbara Bush wig (too bad they didn't spring for a Barbara Bush dress from her favorite designer, Arnold Scaasi), and sang:

Why can't the Bush men use real English when they
    speak?
Their verbal self-destruction is more than tongue-in-cheek.
How could it be that Yalies mangle words the way they
    do?
They *really* went to Skull and Bones U.
Now George W.'s way of speaking has been gaining wide
    attention.
That high horse claiming the low road was his masterful
    invention.

Clear, precise language I'm afraid he'll never get . . .
Oh, *why* can't the Bush men learn to—set a good example
        by stringing nouns and verbs together without
        slips?
Or falling into traps about read-ing lips?
They'd do far better reading Webster's dictionary for
        tips—or coming to me for some very pithy quips!
To use proper English doesn't mean that you're a geek.
Why can't the Bush men,
Why can't my Georges learn *to speak?*

In late February 2001, Bush traveled to Tennessee to pitch his education plan, which he said would see the Education Department grow more than any other federal agency under his proposed budget. He also argued for annual performance tests. "You teach a child to read, and he or her will be able to pass the literary test," he said, bungling his grammar a bit.

Bush later paid a visit to a second-grade class at a school, and a little girl asked her classmate, "That's him?"

"Yeah, that's him," he replied. "Duh!"

British Prime Minister Tony Blair paid a visit to Washington in late February, and he and Bush put their best faces forward to show the beginnings of a cordial relationship. Bush even noted, "We both use Colgate toothpaste."

"They're going to wonder how you know that, George," said Blair.

Tangling at news conferences, Part I, February 22, 2001:

HT: Mr. President, why do you refuse to respect the wall between church and state? And we know that the mixing of religion and government for centuries has led to slaughter. I mean, the very fact our country has stood in good stead by having a separation, why do you break it down?

Bush: Well, I strongly respect the separation of church and state.

HT: Well, you wouldn't have a religious office in the White House if you did.

Bush: I didn't get to finish my answer, in all due respect. I believe that so long as there's a secular alternative available, we ought to allow individuals who we're helping to be able to choose a program that may be run by a faith-based program or will be run by a faith-based program. I understand full well that some of the most compassionate missions of help and aid come out of faith-based programs, and I strongly support the faith-based initiative that we're proposing, because I don't believe it violates the line between the separation of church and state, and I believe it's going to make America a better place.

HT: You are a secular official.

Bush: I agree. I am a secular official.

I thought that Bush should be asked about the program, which many have said attempts to inject religion in government-funded programs. I don't think there is any such thing as crossing the line on questions like this—all questions of public servants are legitimate. A few weeks later, in an interview with Medill News Service, I acknowledged that some reporters thought I had crossed the line in my questions about the White House's faith-based initiative. "But," I told them, "how come they didn't say that when I was asking about Monica Lewinsky?"

When "W" spoke in Portland, Maine, in March 2001, he recalled to the crowd that when he was governor of Texas, he had gone to a dedication for those who'd served in the Pacific Theater during World War II. "It was in central Texas, a little town called Fredericksburg. My mom and dad were there, and Laura, the great first lady of the United States, was there.

"And I was really looking forward to welcoming all the World War II vets. It was a chance to say thanks on behalf of the sons and daughters of the Great Generation. And I said, 'Mr. President'—that was for my dad, who was the head of the parade, and everybody cheered—and I said, 'Mother.' Before I could get out another word, the place went wild. And I said, 'Well, Mother, it's clear the people of Texas love you, and so do I, but you are still telling me what to do after all these years.'

"And a guy in a big cowboy hat moved out in the middle of Main Street and cupped his hands and screamed at the top of his lungs in front of thirty thousand constituents, 'You better listen to her, too, boy.'"

As the laughter died down, Bush told the gathering, "I can assure you that the president of the United States is listening to his mother. Remember that."

Tangling at news conferences, Part II, with press secretary Ari Fleischer on campaign finance reform, March 22, 2001:

HT: The amendment that passed the Senate providing more money to candidates who have wealthy opponents—does the White House support that amendment?

Fleischer: As you know, you saw the president's principles on campaign finance reform, and the president is not going to comment amendment by amendment. He looks forward to taking a look at the campaign finance reform package as it passes the Senate and then as it passes the House, develops in conference. He's looking forward to building bridges so he can sign a good bill into law this year.

HT: And the amendments—you won't comment on the amendments that failed yesterday, which were part of the president's principles, related to paycheck protection and—

Fleischer: Because, also, from the president's point of view, it's the beginning of the process. There are going to be several more actions taken, many more votes to come in the Senate. And the president is closely monitoring campaign finance reform because he wants to get something done this year. And he believes that with a little effort, with a little good work, a little compromise, that campaign finance reform can be signed into law this year.

HT: Even with the failure of those amendments that he supports, he still thinks that we can get—

Fleischer: It's the beginning of the process.

HT: Will he sign a bill if it doesn't have paycheck protection?

Fleischer: The president is looking forward to working together to bring people together so he can sign a bill.

HT: Why would he take that approach on campaign finance and then talk on the patients' bill of rights about bills that he would veto when the bills haven't been introduced yet?

Fleischer: For the exact same—well, several of the bills have been introduced on patients' bill of rights, which is why the president said what he said yesterday. But for the exact same reason—it's perfectly consistent, because his desire is to get things moving in Washington so legislation can be signed into law. In the case of the patients' bill of rights, he obviously is pushing toward the middle. He wants people to come together on patients' bill of rights and get out of the rut that they've been in last year where nothing got done. So he sent a very clear signal about a patients' bill of rights that has strong patient protections and that does not turn patients' rights over to trial lawyers. That way, we can get something signed. And I note this morning that Congressman Charlie Norwood, one of the lead advocates of patients' bill of rights in the Congress, issued a statement saying that the president today—yesterday—solidly aligned himself with the bipartisan House and Senate coalition that has pushed so hard to have new standards apply to every health plan in the country. So the president is looking to build on both campaign finance reform and patients' bill of rights, bipartisan coalitions so he can sign bills into law. And that contrasts with both campaign finance reform and patients' bill of rights in the last Congress. There was so much of an effort—

HT: It was Republican-dominated, and they wouldn't pass anything. So don't give us that stuff.

Fleischer: Helen, the point is—

HT: It didn't pass because the Republicans were not going to allow it to. Either one.

Fleischer: Would you care to come up here? The point is, it didn't get done in the last Congress because nobody pushed for a bipartisan, centrist solution. You had too many pitted camps, both on patients' bill of rights and campaign finance.

HT: Too many compromises would have been demanded, so why do it?

Fleischer: And the president is trying to build that middle ground on both issues. And he's pleased with what he's done and he thinks it's going to help lead to a year in which he can sign both patients' bill of rights and campaign finance reform.

At the 2001 Gridiron, it was my turn to play first lady again. This time I got to be Laura Bush, and my song was to the tune of "Home on the Range":

> Oh, we've got a home where the buffalo roam
> And the gun nuts and Baptists hold sway
> Where football and prayer are both in the air
> I think Double-U likes it that way.
> Our home's near Waco but to Camp David I'd rather go
> 'Cause Crawford's a snore and this ranch life's a bore
> I'm beginning to like Washington's show
> Oh, I plan to stay—clear out of the way
> And if need be pull strings from behind
> I learned this from Bar; it took her real far
> Her real power no one seemed to find.
> I'll talk about books and schmooze with the agents and
>   cooks
> When we go away

The silver will stay
'Cause we're not like those Arkansas schnooks!

A note on that performance: At the rehearsal, which also draws an audience, I was up onstage singing away and felt my skirt start to slip and slide right to the floor. I did my best to hang on to the errant apparel, but by the time I was finished, said skirt was slumping toward my ankles. I didn't know whether to laugh or cry. Hanging on as best as I could, I exited the stage, giving the crowd my best raised-eyebrows glance. I got some laughs, but the next time around, I made sure the skirt was securely in place.

Before Bush's first hundred days were up, press secretary Ari Fleischer got a little annoyed with some of the questions I was asking. "Tell me, Helen," he said, "are we doing anything right?"

"Give me a week and let me get back to you."

Vice President Dick Cheney, who had suffered four heart attacks, had another episode in March 2001 and underwent a procedure to unblock a cardiac artery. He went back to work less than twenty-four hours after leaving the hospital and emphasized that his duties were not impairing his health and denied he was under any stress. "I'm having the time of my life. I enjoy the job very much. I love working for George Bush," he told reporters.

"He looks good, he feels good, and that's good news," said Bush.

Cheney got to work at 7:30 A.M. and held a series of meetings and squeezed in a news conference afterward.

"I've got a job to do; the president asked me to do it," he said. "I'll do it as long as he's comfortable having me do it and I feel like I can make a contribution. I'm sixty years old, but I very much enjoy my job. I have a good time. I don't consider it stressful."

His boss might have considered the attendant publicity a little stressful, though. At a photo session in the Oval Office with Bush and South Korean President Kim Dae Jung, photographers all but ignored the two heads of state and swarmed around Cheney, who was standing to the side.

"Hey, the photo op is over here, guys!" Bush called out.

Tangling at news conferences, Part III, March 29, 2001:

HT: Thank you, sir. Mr. President.

Bush: No, next to next.

HT: If I could just clarify a little.

Bush: Let me rephrase it: you're last.

HT: No problem. We're used to it. Just to clarify on tax cuts.

Bush: Yes?

HT: I wanted to clarify the linkage that you feel is necessary. You have said that you want to have a tax-cut-rate reduction and you also support the efforts to try to do a quick, retroactive tax cut. When you speak of those two things, will you insist upon one package of bills that includes the rate reduction and any kind of quick, short-term stimulus, or would you accept some kind of verifiable promise that they'll get to your tax cuts later?

Bush: That's the old "trust me"?

HT: Yes.

Bush: It is in our nation's best interest to have long-term tax relief. And that has been my focus all along. I'm confident we can have it, get it done. I believe, not only can we get long-term tax relief in place, since our country's running some surpluses in spite of the dire predictions about cash flow, I believe we have an opportunity to fashion an immediate stimulus package as well. The two ought to go hand in hand. Those who think that they can say, "We're only going to have a stimulus package, but let's forget tax relief," misunderestimate our—excuse me—underestimate . . . (Laughter) Just making sure you're paying attention. You were.

* * *

Bush left the grammar gags at home for his first White House Correspondents dinner in April 2001 and put together what he called a "little slide show," using the many family scrapbooks his mother has been compiling over the years. Noting that in his growing-up years Texas was "still a rough-and-tumble frontier," he flashed a picture of himself astride a pony. "This was my favorite horse. He was surefooted, steady. I trusted that horse totally. And here's the really weird part. His name was Dick Cheney."

Bush also proudly pointed out "my actual first-grade report card. Up top, it says George W. Bush. And then notice the final grades on the right: writing, A; reading, A; spelling, A; arithmetic, A; music, A; art, A.

"So my advice is, don't peak too early."

Explaining the Bush syntax for academia: Bush delivered the commencement address at his alma mater on May 21, 2001, and in his speech noted, "I took a class that studied Japanese haiku. Haiku, for the uninitiated, is a fifteenth-century form of poetry, each poem only having seventeen syllables. Haiku is fully understood only by the Zen masters. As I recall, one of my academic advisers was worried about my selection of such a specialized course. He said I should focus on English. I still hear that quite often.

"But my critics don't realize I don't make verbal gaffes. I'm speaking in the perfect forms and rhythms of ancient haiku.

"I did take English here, and I took a class called 'The History and Practice of American Oratory.' . . . And President Levin, I want to give credit where credit is due. I want the entire world to know this: everything I know about the spoken word, I learned right here at Yale."

John F. Kennedy always told young people they should strive for excellence. Receiving his honorary degree at Yale, Bush told the students, "To those of you who received honors, awards, and distinctions, I say well done. And to those C students, I say, you, too, can be president of the United States."

When Kennedy received a Yale honorary degree, he joked that he now had the best of both worlds: a Harvard education and a Yale degree.

On his way home from his speech at Yale University's commencement, President Bush reached across party lines and gave a lift aboard Air Force One to Lanny Davis, one of President Clinton's "scandal spokesmen" from 1996 to 1998, who had fielded questions about everything from campaign finance irregularities to the Lewinsky mess.

Davis, who graduated from Yale in 1967, a year ahead of Bush, was Bush's fraternity brother at Delta Kappa Epsilon.

Aboard Air Force One, Davis popped briefly into the press cabin and said, "Just like old times."

As for Bush, Davis said, "It never surprises me that he can reach out to people even who disagree with him."

Having a president who once owned a baseball team has put sports in the limelight at the White House. On March 30, 2001, Bush welcomed members of the Baseball Hall of Fame to the White House and noted one of the great things about living in the White House: "You don't have to sign up for a baseball fantasy camp to meet your heroes. It turns out, they come here."

Paying tribute to all the familiar faces, he singled out Yankees catcher Yogi Berra for special recognition. "Yogi's been an inspiration to me," he said, "not only because of his baseball skills but, of course, for the enduring mark he left on the English language. Some in the press corps here even think he might be my speechwriter. I don't know if you know, Yogi, but I quoted you when I went to the Congress the other day to deliver my budget address. 'Relieved you made it, we were afraid you might have taken the wrong fork.'"

During the visit, Bush also announced his intention to build a baseball diamond on the South Lawn for Little League play. "In a small way, maybe we can help to preserve the best of baseball right here in the house that Washington built," he said. "After we moved in, I pointed out to a great baseball fan, the first lady, that we've got a pretty good-sized backyard here. And maybe with the help of some groundskeepers, we can play ball on the South Lawn. She agreed, just so long as I wasn't one of the players."

The first T-ball game on the South Lawn occurred in late May between two Washington Little League teams, the Red Sox and the Rockies. Bush led the group in a pregame recitation of the Little League credo: "I will play fair and strive to win, but win or lose, I will always do my best."

Opening day on the South Lawn drew several hundred spectators, and calling the play-by-play was none other than announcer Bob Costas.

No official score was kept, there were lots of errors, and one player had a difficult time finding third base. Although there is no pitcher—batters hit at a ball sitting atop a vertical tube—some balls still ended up behind home plate.

"You'd think the catcher wouldn't see much action in T-ball," Costas noted.

However, even when the talk turns to baseball, a president can sometimes put people to sleep. In early May, Bush was entertaining the New York Yankees in the Oval Office, chatting with owner George Steinbrenner and others, and Yankees vice president Arthur Richman started to nod off and lean over.

As Bush was talking, Steinbrenner suddenly said, "Excuse

me, Mr. President, but you better be careful. You're about to lose your seat."

"Only George Steinbrenner could interrupt the president in midsentence," said Bush.

In honor of the holiday Cinco de Mayo, Bush delivered his Saturday radio address in both English and Spanish. In preparation, press secretary Ari Fleischer noted, "He said he hopes he doesn't butcher the Spanish as badly as he had the English."

In Bush's first months in office, sports figures of all kinds visited the White House. In April, the NCAA men's and women's championship basketball teams, Duke and Notre Dame, had an audience with Bush. When the women's coach, Muffet McGraw, told the president she couldn't yell at the players "because they do everything we ask," Bush told her, "I need your help with Congress."

In March, Bush spoke to the University of Oklahoma Sooners football team and drew some parallels between sports and politics. "We share a lot in common," he told the players. "We both started in our respective campaigns as underdogs. We both won our championships in the state of Florida. . . . There's a big difference, though. It took you all of sixty minutes. It took me thirty-six days."

On October 11, 2001, one month after the devastating terrorist attacks on the World Trade Center and the Pentagon, President Bush held a prime-time news conference. In the question-and-answer session, he did his best to reassure Americans that the United States was on the right track in its retaliatory operations against those responsible and to help us all feel a little less unsettled. He also showed how, in one of the most difficult times in modern history, a little presidential levity always helps, when my question to him and his response garnered a few laughs at the session.

Bush: The actions my government takes in concert with other countries, the actions we take at home to defend ourselves, will serve as a go-by for future presidents or future prime ministers in Britain, for example, or future FBI directors. It is important that we stay the course, bring these people to justice to show—and show others how to fight the new wars of the twenty-first century. Yes, Helen . . .

HT: Mr. President, on that note, we understand you have advisers who are urging you to go after Iraq, take out Iraq, Syria, and so forth. Do you really think that the American people will tolerate you widening the war beyond Afghanistan? And I have a follow-up.

Bush: I knew you would. Thank you for warning me.

A FEW FINAL REFLECTIONS

Former UPI colleague Eliot Brenner, who worked at the Pentagon and on Capitol Hill and later went on to the Federal Aviation Administration, used to draw weekend duty at the White House from time to time when the regular press was traveling with the president. "Every time I had to do the White House," he recalled, "filling in for anyone who was missing, I made it a point to find the press secretary and introduce myself as 'Helen Thomas in drag.' I won't claim it helped, but it sure didn't hurt."

For someone who doesn't drive, Los Angeles can be unnerving and annoying. At the 2000 Democratic National Convention in Los Angeles, getting access to transportation required a little creativity. It was a long walk from the secured area around the convention hall to downtown. Following Monday night's opening session, I got a lift from a friendly police officer in his squad car. The next night, I ran into the mayor's press secretary and asked him where was the closest place I could get a cab. He summoned a nearby fire truck and I climbed aboard. In an interview later, I told the reporter, "I sat in the seat behind the driver and wore a headset in case a fire alarm came in."

Well, the reporter asked, did I have any plans to commandeer a hook and ladder, or a helicopter or an ambulance the next night?

"Who knows?" I said.

* * *

In June 2000, I spoke at a National Press Club luncheon that marked the twenty-fifth anniversary of women journalists joining the organization. At the question-and-answer session, someone sent up a query that was read out loud: "Helen, in your opinion, which first couple has had the best marriage?"

All I could do was put out my hands, palms up, shrug my shoulders, and say, "How would *I* know?"

In the spring of 2001, I was asked to deliver the commencement address at Mississippi University for Women. Another guest was former CNN chief Ted Turner.

"How many honorary degrees do you have?" he asked me.

"Oh, maybe thirty-one," I said.

"I've got thirty-two."

"Well, who's counting?"

In May 2001, the American News Women's Club held its annual benefit banquet, and the designated "roastee" was Al Neuharth, the man behind *USA Today* and a pioneer of modern journalism. Al also received the first annual award given by the club for lifetime achievement in journalism, an award they had graciously named for me. When Al was presented with the trophy—two question marks fitted onto a wood base—he remarked how fitting the award was and told a story that surprised even me:

"I had the chance to interview Fidel Castro once," he recalled, "and during our conversation I asked him, 'Mr. President, what is the biggest difference between being the president of Cuba and being the president of the United States?'

"Castro didn't even blink:

" 'I don't have to answer questions from Helen Thomas.' "

Memo to Regis Philbin:

On July 6, 2000, a number of people called to let me know I'd been included in the popular TV show *Who Wants to Be a Millionaire*. The question was "What part of government does Helen Thomas cover?"

The White House, of course—and that's my final answer.

EPILOGUE

I love to laugh and I have appreciated the times when I could laugh with a president—or laugh at him.

At the White House, life is real, life is earnest, and we need a sense of humor to lighten the load.

It works both ways. Reporters and photographers also need a sense of humor and the ability to laugh. Watching history from a ringside seat is often painful. Historic events are not funny. Grim and horrifying is sometimes a better way to put it. And for reporters at the scene, there are more things to cry than to laugh about.

So we cherish and wallow in the times that we come together to enjoy a good laugh.

I hope future presidents see it that way, too.

ACKNOWLEDGMENTS

Thanks for the Memories, Mr. President never could have been written without the superb support of my editor/researcher Kathleen Silvassy—who also provided some levity in this long undertaking with her wry but rather astute observations of the Washington scene. An editor at *Congressional Quarterly*, she helped me scour the past and the present for the high points, low points, foibles, and fun I've been privileged to witness in my years at the White House, on the campaign trail, and in the hometowns of presidents.

I also deeply appreciate the contributions of my agent, Diane Nine, and her family. I am eternally grateful to Lisa Drew of Scribner, who has the brand name when it comes to presidential memoirs and a patent on patience. Her guidance was invaluable.

Sara Sanders, a fellow journalist and master's candidate at George Washington University, came through on several research assignments.

I also relied on the excellent recall and memorabilia of my former UPI White House colleague Al Spivak when it came to shared experiences in the White House. Former UPI colleagues named throughout the text and who have my thanks are Ira Allen, Bill Cotterell, Ron Cohen, Kyle Thompson, Tony Heffernan, Sue Morgan, Eliot Brenner, Mark Ridolfi, Gene Hintz, Jim Wieck, Tom Foty, Mark Ridolfi, Dave Rosen, and Dick Taffe.

Joe Laitin, who worked for UPI many, many years ago and went on to greater glory as a spokesman extraordinaire through five administrations at the White House and the Pentagon and is a walking encyclopedia, got used to my calls for bits of information. The hilarious anecdotes about Lyndon B. Johnson recounted in *LBJ* by the late Frank Cormier, White House correspondent for the Associated Press, helped bring back those incredible days in the 1960s. C. Landon Parvin helped me immeasurably with current White House history. I am also indebted to Hassan Yassin for his knowledge, friendship, and encouragement over the years.

There is no way I can repay my family for their love and constancy these many years, including my sisters Isabelle, Josephine, and Barbara and my brother Matry. Anne Thomas, Kate Mabarak, Genevieve Parker, and Sabe Thomas, my sisters and brother who have passed on, will never be forgotten for their everlasting devotion to all of us.

I count among my blessings my close family, and I have been so fortunate to have nieces and nephews—and their spouses—who have always been there for me. A special thanks to my Washington-based contingent, niece Terri De Leon and her husband, Yuri, and Judy Jenkins and her husband, Tim. Their talented young children—Genevieve De Leon and Jack, Michael, and Isabelle Jenkins—have been a special joy.

And when the book-writing chores bordered on procrastination, a trip home to Detroit would give me a new perspective and a chance to see my other nieces and nephews and their families, who all make me very proud.

INDEX

"Helen Thomas is not only one of the smartest and savviest Washington reporters ever, she's also one of the most admired, and *Front Row at the White House* tells you why."

—Dan Rather, CBS News

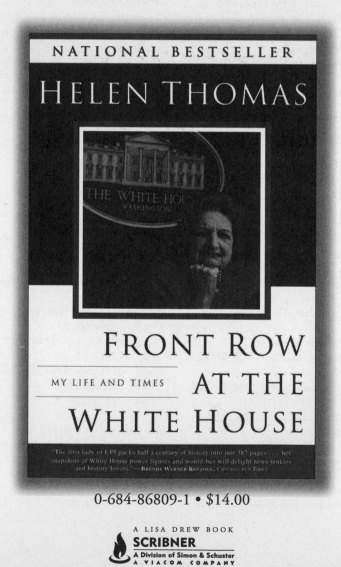